Australia's Oldest Wreck

The historical background and archaeological analysis of the wreck of the English East India Company's ship *Trial*, lost off the coast of Western Australia in 1622

Jeremy N. Green

BAR Supplementary Series 27
1977

British Archaeological Reports

122, Banbury Road, Oxford OX2 7BP, England

GENERAL EDITORS

A. C. C. Brodribb, M.A.
Mrs. Y. M. Hands

A. R. Hands, B.Sc., M.A., D.Phil.
D. R. Walker, M.A.

B.A.R. Supplementary Series, 27, 1977: "Australia's Oldest Wreck: the loss of the Trial, 1622".
© Jeremy N. Green, 1977.

ISBN 9780904531770 paperback
ISBN 9781407344249 e-book
DOI https://doi.org/10.30861/9780904531770
A catalogue record for this book is available from the British Library
This book is available at www.barpublishing.com

CONTENTS

LIST OF ILLUSTRATIONS

1. INTRODUCTION

In 1621, the English East India Company dispatched the ship <u>Trial</u> to the Indies; during her outward voyage in May the following year she was wrecked on a reef off the coast of Western Australia, thus becoming the earliest known ship to be lost in Australian waters. Discovered in 1969, the <u>Trial</u> is also the earliest known wreck of an East Indiaman to have been discovered so far. The following chapters deal with the historical background to the loss and the modern identification of the wrecksite.

The <u>Trial</u> was lost as a result of a navigational error on the part of her Master, who had been instructed to follow a new course to the Indies. The English Company had learned a few years earlier of a new fast route to the Indies that their rivals, the Nederlandse Verenigde Oost-Indische Compagnie, had discovered. This route had been pioneered in 1611, and took an easterly course from the Cape of Good Hope, and then a northerly one to the Indies. Following this course some Nederlandse ships had sailed too far to the east and, as a result, in 1616, the coast of Western Australia was discovered. There were numerous sightings of this land in the years that followed. Navigators of the time were faced with several problems, both because of uncertainty of the position of the land and the related difficulty in determining the ship's longitude. Inevitably ships ran into difficulties by coming unexpectedly on this coast, particularly at night. It is indeed surprising that of all the ships that sailed to the Indies in the 17th and 18th centuries, only five are known to have been lost on this coast, (see Sigmond and Zuiderbaan, 1976), the <u>Trial</u> on a remote reef off the NW coast.

In the débâcle that followed, more than 100 men were lost, as well as most of the Company's goods. Subsequently, there were serious allegations against the Master: that he was negligent; that he had stolen some of the Company's goods; that he was an incompetent navigator. Examinations of the records seem to indicate that the Master falsified the location of the rocks to make it appear that he had been following orders, and so absolving himself of responsibility. Thus Trial Rocks remained undiscovered for over 300 years, simply because they were not where they were said to be.

The subsequent career of the Master is of interest especially as the events reflect on his honesty. On the basis of his false statements he was acquitted by the Company of any blame, and was then given the command of the East Indiaman <u>Moone</u>, in which he returned home in 1624. In 1625, the <u>Moone</u> was wrecked off Dover. The Master was immediately put in prison in Dover Castle for purposely wrecking the ship. The court case dragged on for two years; finally he made a supplicative petition to the Company and the case was dropped.

By the 18th century, there was complete confusion in the charts as to the position of Trial Rocks. At least four groups of non-existent islands were charted in the area, and it was not until the advent of accurate longitude determination and the Admiralty Hydrographic Surveys in the late 18th and early 19th century that these anachronisms were sorted out. Initially, the Admiralty officially declared Trial Rocks non-existent. Later their position was rather arbitrarily assigned to a group of islands in the general area. In 1934, Lee published the Master's letters which showed that a reef known as Ritchie's Reef was in fact the reef on which the Trial was lost. The Australia Pilot was amended and so finally Trial Rocks were officially and correctly located 314 years after their first tragic discovery.

In 1969, an expedition was mounted to locate the wrecksite of the Trial. On the first day of the search around the rocks, a wrecksite was located, and tentatively identified as that of the Trial. Although three expeditions have visited the site since, no evidence has been found to conclusively identify the site. Circumstantial evidence indicates that the wrecksite is that of the Trial and at present there is nothing to contradict it.

2. THE ROUTE TO THE INDIES

When the Old or London East India Company, (E.E.I.C., formed in 1600), and the Nederlandse Verenigde Oost-Indische Compagnie (V.O.C., formed in 1602), sent their first fleets to the Indies, they followed the route pioneered by the Portuguese (fig. 1). After doubling the Cape of Good Hope, the ships sailed along the east coast of Africa, passed Natal and through the Mozambique Channel, and then across the Indian Ocean to the Indies. Later, due to problems with their rivals, the Portuguese, ships took a course to the east of Madagascar, to avoid the Portuguese stronghold at Mozambique.

However it soon became obvious that there were many grave objections to this route. The prevailing south-easterly trade winds and the southerly Mozambique Current made it difficult to sail north along the East coast of Africa. In the hot equatorial areas, there were often long periods when ships were becalmed, causing provisions to rot and crews to sicken. Also there were numerous shoals, islands and reefs in the central Indian Ocean, causing navigational hazards.

In 1610, the V.O.C. pioneered a new route to the Indies. Hendrik Brouwer, a bewindhebber (director) and later Gouverneur Generaal of the V.O.C. in the Indies, after his return from the Indies in 1610, suggested a new route from the Cape of Good Hope to the Indies. He suggested that it might be of advantage to utilise the westerly winds that prevail in the latitudes between 35 and 40°S. In December 1610, the Heren XVII dispatched Brouwer in the Roode Leeuw met Pijlen in company with the ships Gouda and Veere with instructions to investigate this route. After leaving the Cape of Good Hope, Brouwer first sailed south until the westerlies were encountered in about 36°S., then he sailed east until it was estimated that they were in the meridian of the Straits of Sunda, where they turned north. This new route took less than six months, compared with a year or more for the older route. On his arrival, Brouwer advocated the new route, outlining the many advantages to the Heren XVII. Before adopting this route and issuing general sailing instructions, the Heren XVII issued further orders for other ships to investigate it. Pieter de Carpentier, who was ordered to follow this route, reported:

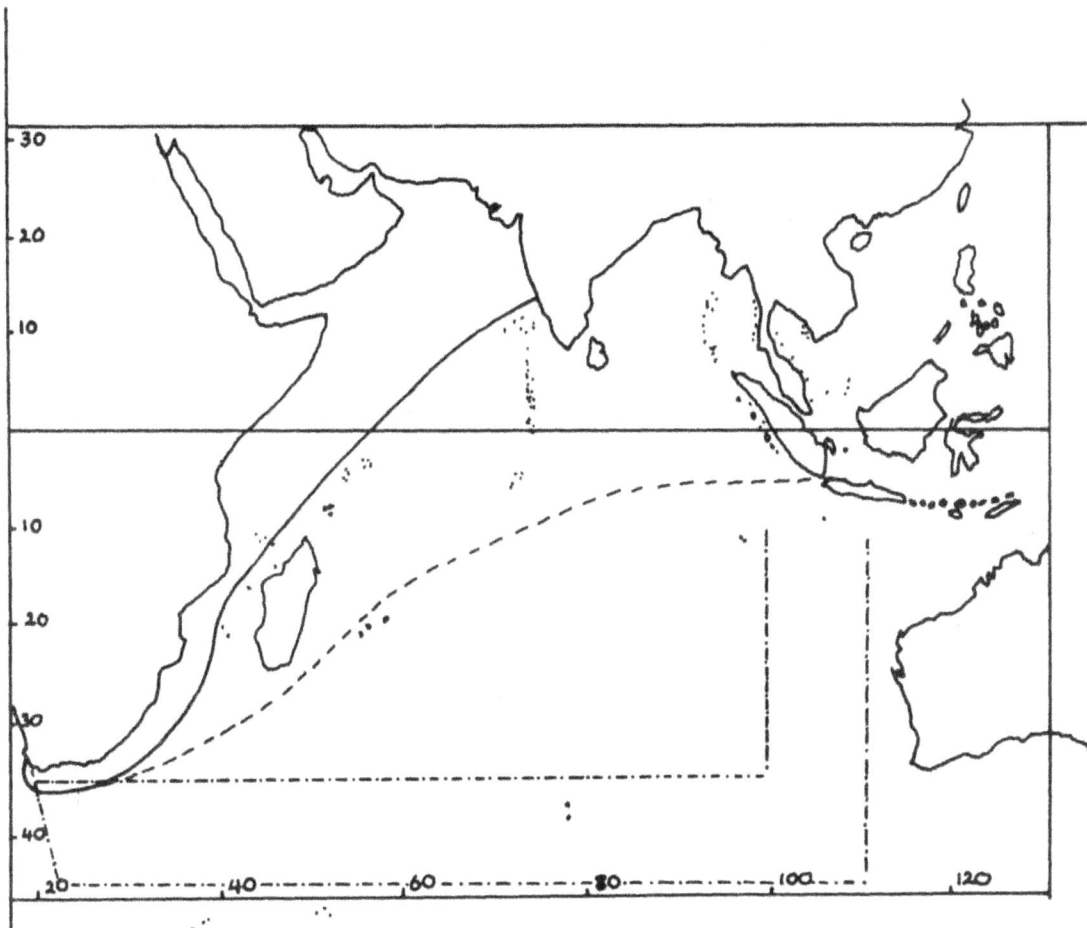

Fig. 1   Routes to the Indies east of the Cape of Good Hope, showing early
         Portuguese and V.O.C. route (_____), later V.O.C. route
         (--------) and Brouwer Route (-.-.-.-.).

"And if we had to sail a hundred times to the Indies we should
use no other route than this. It ensures the [maintenance in]
good condition of trade goods and provisions,and a healthy crew
besides" (Schilder 1976).

Jan Pieterzoon Coen, the Gouverneur Generaal in the Indies stressed the desirability of this route, and in August 1616 the Heran XVII resolved that:

"The ships leaving here must follow on their outward voyage
the course described by Jan Pieterzoon Coen in his latest letters
and by commandeur Brouwer in his discourse, and by which
route many ships have travelled much more quickly; and for
better care and attention of the above order, a reward for a
voyage to Bantam of less than seven, eight and nine months
respectively will be payed. It is to be understood that the koopman, schipper and stuyrman of the ships that call into any
other place than Tafelbaey (unless in an emergency) whereby
delaying their voyage, will have to pay an amends of six hundred
guilders to the profits of the Company." (van Dam, 1701)

By 1617 the V.O.C. had published the Seijnbrief or Seijlaesorders, (sailing
instructions), which incorporated the Brouwer Route, (fig. 2).

Article 12 states: "And all ships will, after having taken refreshments
at the Cape de Bona Esperance or Tafelbay, put their course east in the latitude 35,36,40 to 44 degrees South, so that they will find the best westerly
winds, also because these winds blow not always at the latitude of 35 or 36
but often more southerly, they should be looked for there."

Article 13: "Having found the westerly winds, the ships shall keep an
easterly course at least for 1000 mijlen (for the length of the mijl see below)
before they move upwards or make their course northerly, the Javanese
coast, is not further than $7\frac{1}{2}^{0}$ southward, so that because of this precision
one should fear nothing; but by crossing before one reaches 1000 mijlen, there
is the danger of getting on the coast of Sumatra, where because of the S.E.
winds that are there between April and October, one will have to beat against
the wind for a long time."

Article 14: "This course we think better than the others inside or outside
Madagskar near the equator, not only because in this course there is open sea,
free from rocks and shoals, but it is much cooler and for the people much
healthier and presenting less rotting and decay of the provisions and loaded
goods, [better climate], but also because here there are constantly blowing
westerly winds, and because the degrees are importantly smaller, one makes
up for in this course by looking for the westerly winds and going to the north
again, largely what one seems to lose." (Stapel, 1937).

Not all V.O.C. ships followed the sailing orders. Willem Ysbrantsz
Bontekoe, for example, sailed to the east of Madagascar on his voyage to
the Indies in 1618 in the Nieuw Hoorn. Bontekoe relates that the ship
Enkhuiksen sailed to the west of Madagaskar, as she was bound for the coast
of Coromandel. It should be noted this was the year after the publication of

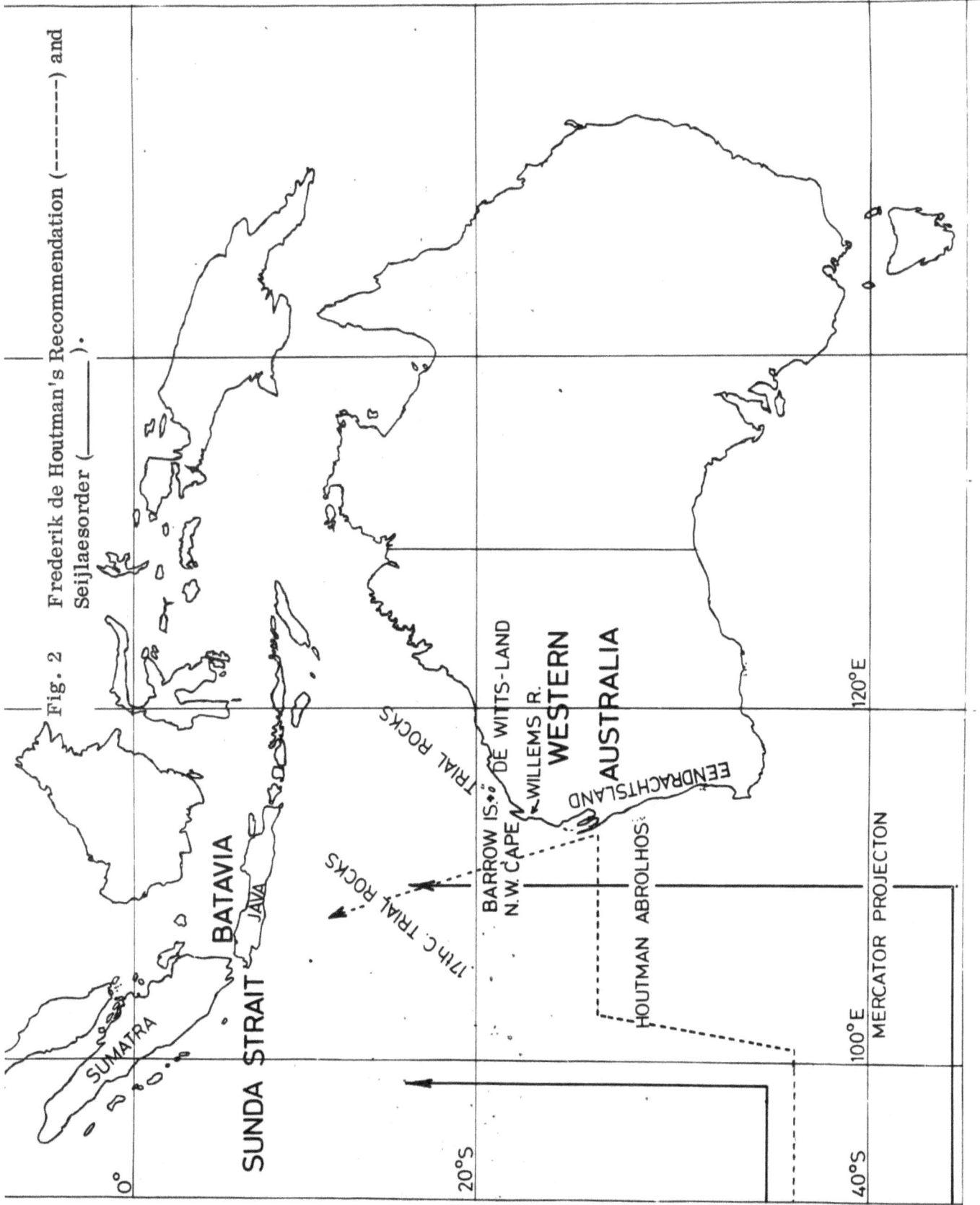

Fig. 2   Frederik de Houtman's Recommendation (- - - - - -) and Seijlaesorder (————).

the V.O.C. seijlaesorder. Bontekoe records that on this 'old' course the crew suffered considerably from sickness, and he was forced to stop at Madagaskar, then go south to Mauritius, and finally back to St. Maria near Madagaskar for refreshment. From there Bontekoe sailed south to lat. 33°S, veered eastward and set his course for the Straits of Sunda, taking almost a year to reach the Indies, (Bontekoe 1646).

3. SIGHTING OF THE GREAT SOUTHLAND PRIOR TO 1622

It was inevitable that ships sailing on the Brouwer Route would eventually happen upon the west coast of Australia. According to the seijlaesorder, sailing 1,000 mijlen east from the Cape of Good Hope in latitude 45°S would put a ship in longitude 112°E. If the ships sailed north from this point, the Southland would have been in almost the same longitude as the westernmost point of the Southland, (113°E). In fact the instructions are curious since although mentioning the difference in the length of a degree of longitude in different latitudes, this difference is not taken into account. Accordingly, if a ship sailed 1,000 mijlen in 35°S, it would be in longitude 101°E, further west than sailing the same distance in latitude 45°S (fig. 2). However, differences in the length of the mijl complicate this problem, see below.

The first sighting of the west coast of the Southland was in 1616 by the ship Eendracht skippered by Dirck Hatichs (Hartogszoon). De Houtman states that the Eendracht encountered land between 25°S. and 22°S, and this was subsequently named Eendrachtsland. The first landfall of the Eendracht was on an island in latitude 25°S, where a pewter plate was erected on a post, commemorating the new discovery. The inscription read "A.D. 1616, on the 25th October [new style] there arrived here the ship d'Eendracht van Amsterdam the opperkopman Gilles Miebais van Luck, Schipper Dirck Hatichs van Amsterdam the 27 dito sailed to Bantum, the ondercoepman Jan Stins the opperstuierman Pietr Doores van Bil Anno 1616." (The history of the discovery of this plate by Willem de Vlamingh in 1697 is given in Halls, (1964) and Schilder, (1976)). The island on which Hatichs landed is now known as Dirck Hartog's Island, and the landfall marked the beginning of occasional encounters with the coast by ships outward bound for the Indies (fig. 3).

In May 1618, the V.O.C. ship Seewolff came upon the newly discovered (but to those on board, still unknown) land. The opperkoopman Pieter Dirkszoon wrote to the Bewindhebbers of the V.O.C.: "Having on the 11th May [new style] reached 21°15'S latitude we saw and discovered ... land about 5 or 6 mijlen to windward east of us, which in consequence we were unable to touch at ... we do not know whether it forms an unbroken coastline or is made up of separate islands. In the former case it might well be a mainland coast for it extended to a very great length. But only the Lord knows the real state of affairs. At all events it would seem never to have been made or discovered by anyone before us, as we have never heard such discovery; and the chart shows nothing but open ocean at this place. According to our schipper's estimation in his chart the Straet van Sunda was then N.N.E. of us at about 250 mijlen distance; according to our onderstuijrman's reckoning the direction was N.E., and according to the opperstuijrman's estimation N.E. by N. These statements, however, proved erroneous since we arrived

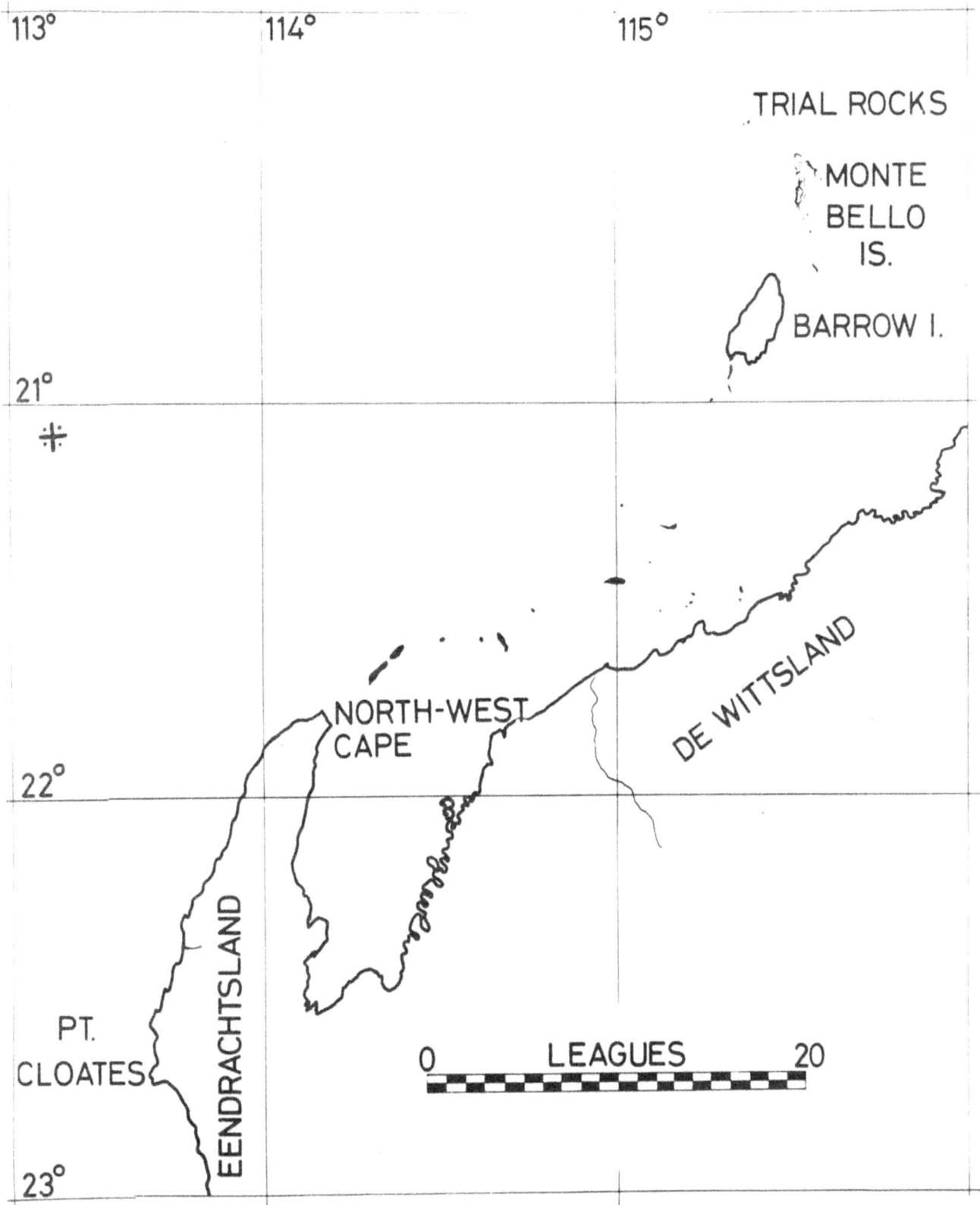

113° 114° 115°

TRIAL ROCKS

MONTE
BELLO
IS.

BARROW I.

21°

NORTH-WEST
CAPE

DE WITTSLAND

22°

EENDRACHTSLAND

PT.
CLOATES

0 LEAGUES 20

23°

Fig. 3   North-western coast of Australia, showing Trial Rocks and the
         position of the Trial on the 24 May (marked thus ☀), the day
         before the loss.

east of Bali on a N.N.E. course so that this land bears the Straet van Sunda N.N.W. (note Heeres is erroneous here, claiming S.S.W.), and ships must arrive in Java eastward of the Straet van Sunda on a north-by-west or northern course." Heeres, (1899): 8A. The schipper of the Seewolff, Haevick Claeszoon van Hillegom, also wrote in a similar vein noting that "the compass has one point north westerly variation here". Heeres, (1899): 8B.

Willem Jansz, the koopman on board the V.O.C. ship Mauritius, indicated in a letter to the V.O.C. that his ship had also come upon the Southland: "On the 31st July (1618) [new style], we discovered an island and landed on the same, where we found the marks of human footsteps; on the west side it extends N.N.E. and S.S.W.; it measures 15 mijlen in length and its northern extremity is in 22°S lat." Heeres, (1899): 9. This is more than likely N.W. Cape which was subsequently marked on charts as an island. This is the same 'island' that Brookes (the Master of the Trial) reports in 22° as "formilie seene by ye flemings". He stated the island was 18 leagues long which is very close to the reckoning of Jansz.

The next sighting of the Southland was by Commandeur Frederik de Houtman in 1619: "We next sailed from Tafelbay with the ships Dordrecht and Amsterdam on June the 8th [new style] ... We ran on with a fair north-west wind as far as 36°30', in which latitude we kept this steady breeze with us up to the 17th of July [new style], when we estimated ourselves to have sailed straight to the east-ward the space of a thousand mijlen. We observed 16° decreasing north-westerly variation of the compass, and resolved to steer... on a north-east-by-north course, we then being in 35°25' Southern Latitude. After keeping the aforesaid course for about 60 mijlen, in the evening of the 19th, we suddenly saw land which we steered away from .... On the 29th do. deeming ourselves to be in an open sea, we shaped our course north-by-east. At noon we were in 29°32' S.Lat.; at night about three hours before daybreak, we again unexpectedly came upon a low-lying coast, a level, broken country with reefs all around it. We saw no high land or mainland, so that this shoal is to be carefully avoided as very dangerous to ships that wish to touch at this coast. It is fully ten mijlen in length lying in 28°46'."

"On the 2nd August [new style], ... we turned our course eastward; at noon we again sighted a long stretch of land in Lat. 27°40'S. We are all assured that this is the land which the ship Eendracht discovered and made in the year [left blank] and noways doubt that all the land they saw in 22, 23, 25 degrees, and which we sighted down to 33 degrees is one uninterrupted mainland coast."

"When in 26°20', we were in sight of land, we had 8° decreasing north-westerly variation of the compass. We then shaped our course north and north by west, which leaves it due north, if the variation is deducted. On the 29th August [new style] we made the south coast of Java, 60 mijlen to eastwards of the westerly extremity of the said island, so that if you are near this South-land in 23, 24 or 25 degrees S. Lat., and shape your course north by west, which deducting the variation is due north-north-west, you will strike the coast of Java [left blank] mijlen eastward of its south-western extremity. Therefore, in order to have a fixed course from the Caep to Java, it is advisable to set sail from the Caep de bonne Esperance in June or July and to run on an eastern course in 36 and 37 degrees Southern Latitude, until you estimate yourself to have covered a thousand mijlen to eastward, after which you had better shape your course north and north by east, until you get into 26 or 27 degrees, thus shunning the shoal aforesaid which lies off the South-land in 28°46'. (The Houtman Abrolhos, as it was later known.)

"When you have reached the 26th or 27th degree, run eastward until you come in sight of the South-land, and then, as before mentioned, from there hold your course north by west and north-north-west, and you are sure to make the western extremity of Java." Heeres, (1899): 11B, (see fig. 2).

4. NAVIGATIONAL PROBLEMS RELATED TO THE BROUWER ROUTE

With the discovery of Eendrachtsland, skippers and steersmen had to pay particular attention to accurately determining their position when following the Brouwer Route. It was obviously dangerous to sail too far to the east and thus come unwittingly on the Southland. To appreciate the magnitude of this problem, and the reasons behind the loss of the Trial, it is necessary to discuss briefly the methods of navigation that were used at the time.

The navigator, departing from a known point, would observe his latitude, (if this were possible), and prick the position on the chart. The following noon he would observe his latitude, and estimate the distance that he had sailed in the last 24 hours. With the distance and course, he would prick his new position. This process was repeated day by day; should his observed latitude differ from his latitude estimated by dead reckoning, this would be corrected. Thus it is not surprising that the longitude, which was determined by estimation alone, and could not be checked by measurement, tended to become more and more inaccurate as the voyage progressed.

The three essential components of this type of mavigation were to determine the latitude, the course sailed, and the distance covered. Latitude could be determined fairly accurately using an astrolabe, quadrant, cross-staff (Jacob's Staff), back-staff (Davis' Quadrant) or semi-circular astrolabe. It is known from the will of Thomas Bonner, who was Master of the Expedition in the E.E.I.C. fleet that sailed to the Indies under the command of Captain William Keeling in 1615, that he owned one or more types of quadrant, a cross-staff, a back-staff, an astrolabe, and celestial and terrestial globes. (Strachan and Penrose, 1971.) From the excavation of the V.O.C. ship Batavia, which was lost in 1629, it is known that she carried at least three sea-astrolabes, a semi-circular astrolabe, an astrolabium catholicum, and a globe (Green, 1975). In 1673 the V.O.C. published a list of navigation equipment for the skipper of the ship Ternate, and it includes a bronze sea-astrolabe, a semi-circular astrolabe, a 'Graedboogh' (Jacob's Staff), a 'Hoeckboogh' (Davis' Quadrant), and an astrolabium catholicum (Mörzer Bruyns and Schilder, 1974). The accuracy of the latitude observations using these instruments was good, as can be seen from the charts of the time, for example Samuel Volkersen plotted the position of Rottnest Island in 1658 from the Wackende Boey, (a V.O.C. vessel sent in search of the Vergulde Draeck), within 6' of its true position, (Green, 1973). Thus from the average of the observations of the height of the Sun taken by the officers at noon, and by using tables of the declination of the Sun that were commonly available at the time, (e.g. Blaeu, 1612), the latitude could be determined.

The course was determined with a compass, however the navigator had to be aware of variation and leeway. Three methods of determining the variation were available at the time: the bearing of the Sun or pole star at their meridian transit, this was inaccurate and only used for approximate determinations; the equal altitude bearing system was popular in the late 16th century, the Sun being observed twice on the same day at the same altitude, the mean of the difference between the two bearings giving the variation, this method takes no account of the change in the declination between the times of the two readings, nor if the ship is moving the difference between the positions of the two observations; the amplitude system relies on tables for calculating the variation from the bearing of the Sun at sun-rise or sun-set. The latter system was attractive as it required only one observation. Tables were published by Hariot in 1594, and there is record of its use by the Masters Mate Nathaniel Marten of the E.E.I.C. ship Globe, (Captain Anthony Hippon), off Java in 1612.

The determination of variation enabled the navigator to correct his course to true north, this was often done by adjusting the compass card, and also as an attempted method for determining longitude. It had long been hoped that variation could be used as a method for determining longitude, but the paucity of observations and the difficulty in determining variation accurately on board ship made this technique impractical for general navigation. Gellibrand in 1633 discovered the secular change in variation, which showed the theoretical aspects of the proposed methods of determining longitude by variation were based on unsound principals. Variation was however still a useful method of determining approximate longitude, and its use continued into the late 18th century up to the introduction of the Harrison chronometer. In the case of the East Indies trade where it was possible to provide regular annual observations of the variation it was a particularly useful method of determining the approximate longitude, and there is no doubt that the knowledge of the variation was used as a check on the easting and westing made by ships.

Leeway also had to be taken into account when determining the course, generally a weighted line was streamed astern and the angle of leeway observed with a compass, and thus the course could be corrected, (Wagenaar, 1583).

The distance that the ship sailed was determined either by a log-line, Dutchman's log, or by estimation based on experience. The log-line was said to have been invented by the English in the 1570s, and was first described by Bourne (1580). Mainwayring in his Seaman's Dictionary describes the "logg-line" as follows: "... some call this a Minut-line; it is a small line with a little peece of a boord at the end, with a little lead to it, to keepe it edg-long in the water; the use of it is, that by judging how many faddome this runs out in a Minut, to give a judgment how many leagues the ship will run in a watch, for if in a minut there run out 14 faddom of the line, then they conclude that the ship doth run a mile in an houre, (for 60 (the number of minuts in a howre) being multiplied by 14 (the number of faddome) make just as many places as are in a mile) so accordingly, as in a minut, there runs out more or lesse, they doe by judgement allow for the Ships way; but this is a way of no certainty, unlesse the wind and seas, and the course would continue all one; besides the error in turning the Glasse, and stopping the line both in an instant, so that it is rather to be esteemed as a trick for a conclusion, then any sollid way to ground upon....", Mainwayring (1644). Several 17th century navigators cast doubts on the use of the log-line, notably Smith (1627), who stated: "... some use a Log line, and a minute glasse to know what way shee makes, but that is so uncertaine, it is not worth the labour to trie it." In spite of the doubts expressed about the log-line, it was commonly used by the English on voyages to the Indies in the first quarter of the 17th century. Captain William Keeling on his second voyage to the Indies in 1607, (the third voyage of the E.E.I.C. to the Indies), in the Dragon, recorded: "... I hoysted out my Sckiffe, and sent her to ride neere us to prove the set of the Current: she found by the Log-line, the Current to set South-east by East two miles a watch, howbeit the Sckiffe roade wind-road...." (Waters, 1958). Captain Antony Hippon, on his voyage to the Indies in 1612, in the Globe, also records in his journal running by the "logge", (Purchas, 1625).

The Dutchman's log consisted of two marks on the side of the ship at a known distance apart; a chip of wood was thrown into the water and the time it took to pass between the two fixed marks was measured. Gunter (1623), mentions the use of a watch, minute-glass, counting one's pulse, or repeating a certain number of words, as methods of measuring the time. This system was inconvenient as it was unlikely that watches were commonly available, the minute-glass was only good for measuring a fixed time and not a variable one, and the latter two systems were inaccurate. A further problem was that the wake around the side of a ship did not necessarily reflect the true speed of a ship through the water. Waters (1958), has suggested that the Dutchman's log may have been invented by Gunter as he was the first to describe it (Gunter, 1623), and as it was not mentioned in any Nederland work until 1662. It is interesting to note that the Dutchman's log was still being used by the V.O.C. in 1789, Captain Bligh on his return to England on a V.O.C. ship noted that "the company do not allow it. Their manner of computing their run, is by means of a measured distance of 40 feet, along the ship's side: they take notice of any remarkable patch of froth, when it is abreast the foremost end of the measured distance, and count half seconds till the mark of froth is abreast the after end. With the number of half seconds thus obtained, they divide the number 48, taking the product for the rate of sailing in geographical miles in one hour, or the number of Dutch miles in four hours." (Irving, 1936).

The reluctance of navigators to adopt the log-line may have been due to the uncertainty of the length of the degree, certainly it was the source of considerable error. By the end of the 16th century most European countries had their own local measurements, and their own relationship of these measurements to the degree. In most cases the length of the degree was related to calculations made by Eratosthenes (c. 267-196 B.C.), Posidonius (135-50 B.C.) and Ptolemy in the 2nd century A.D. In England at the end of the 16th century it was generally considered that there were 5000 feet in a nautical mile, that 3 nautical miles equalled a league, and that 20 leagues made a degree, as a result the length of the nautical mile was underestimated by 17.8%, thus the length of the degree was 1795.6 metres short of the true value. Mainwayring, who wrote his Seaman's Dictionary between 1620 and 1623, advocated 302400 feet in a degree, from the fact that 14 fathoms in a minute gave a nautical mile per hour, (see above). This is a convenience, since the value based on 300000 feet in the degree is 13.89 fathoms.

In Nederland there were numerous different units of measurement, based on local voet (foot) and duim (inch). The two most commonly used were the Rijnland voet made up of 12 Rijnland duim, and the Amsterdam voet made up of 11 Amsterdam duim. Norwood (1637) gives the Rhynland foot as 1.033 times the English, and the Amsterdam foot 0.934 times the English, i.e. 0.31486 m and 0.28468 m respectively. Van IJk (1697) indicates that the Rijnland and Amsterdam duim were equal, however at a later date these two units are given different values, (Rijnland duim = 2.616 cm and Amsterdam duim = 2.537 cm, (van Dale, 1970). Van IJk also lists Mechlse voet (10 duim), Luyxe voet (10 duim), Weselsche voet (11 duim), Maastrigtse voet (10 duim), s'Hertogen Bosch voet (10 duim), Hollands palmen, and Parikse voet. In the 16th century in Nedlerland, the mijl (mile) was the old Duitsche mijl, and 15 of these were considered to make a degree, it was considered that there were 18912 Amsterdam voet in the Duitsche mijl. This value was even more inaccurate than the English value, being 27.8% short of the true value.

The length of the degree was re-determined in Nederland by Willebrord Snellius in 1615 and published in 1617. He showed that there were 22800 Rijnland voet in a Duitsche mijl, (Snellius, 1617), and thus indicated the errors in the then current values of the length of the degree. Gunter (1623) advocated the new Snellius determination of 352347 English feet in a degree, suggesting a modified value of 352000 English feet in a degree. Later, in 1637, Norwood published a new English determination of 367196 (or for convenience 367200) feet in the degree (Norwood, 1637). Stapel (1937) notes that the Amsterdam kaartenmaker Willem Janszoon Blaeu made a very accurate determination of the degree around 1617, but that it was never published. The following table lists the various values of the length of the degree for the first half of the 17th century, and indicates the errors.

16th century English	300000 English feet	91440 metres	- 17.8%
16th century Nederland	283680 Amst. voet	80280 metres	- 27.8%
Snellius, 1617	342000 Rijn. voet	107388 metres	- 3.4%
Blaeu, c. 1617	?	111210 metres	+ 0.02%
Gunter (Snellius), 1623	352347 English feet	107395 metres	- 3.4%
Gunter revised	352000 English feet	107290 metres	- 3.5%
Norwood, 1637	367196 English feet	111921 metres	+ 0.6%
Norwood revised	367200 English feet	111923 metres	+ 0.6%
True value	364799 English feet	111191 metres	-

It is unlikely that any of the new determinations really caught on in the first half of the 17th century, and it would seem that the V.O.C. seijlaesorder, in their instructions to sail 1000 mijlen east of the Cape of Good Hope in latitude between 35 and 44 degrees, are referring to the old Duitsche mijl. Therefore the estimated longitude would be about 28% short of the true value, and Eendrachtsland would be plotted on the charts with this error.

5. THE CHARTS OF THE TIME

In the 17th century there were two types of charts available, the plane and the Mercator. If the navigator was using a plane chart yet another error was introduced. In the plane charts, the distances between the meridians at every latitude were considered equal to their distance apart at the Equator, so that land masses in high latitudes appeared too far apart. By the end of the 16th century, the errors involved in the use of plane charts had been pointed out by several learned navigators. Martin Cortes' work which was translated from Spanish into English c. 1569 states: "The Plane Cardes are Imperfect. The Pilots and Mariners neither use nor have the knowledge to use other Cardes than onely these that are playne, I have sayde the which because they are not Globus, Spherical or rounde [they] are imperfect, and faile to shewe the true distances. For in howe much they depart from the Equinoctiall towards whyche soever of the Poles the Meridian lynes are contracte[d] narrower and narrower. In such a manner that if two cities or poyntes in the Equinoctiall should be distant of longitude 60 leagues and in the self-same meridian[s] at 60 degrees from the Equinoctiall toward eyther Pole shoulde bee other two Cities or Poyntes they shoulde bee distant in longitude but only 30 leagues. And for the better declaration and understanding hereof, I say that if two shyppes shoulde depart from the Equinoctiall, the one distant from the other 100 leagues by East and West and that eyther of them shoulde sayle directly by his meridian towarde the North then when either of them hath the pole over his horizon 60 degrees, the one shall be distaunt from the other onely 50 leagues by the paralelle of East and West, <u>as appeareth by the playne cardes that they have the self-same hundred leagues</u>. And beside these considerations one errour bringeth in another, so another: where of to speake any more heere it shall be to certeyne Pilots (as ye proverbe saith) not onely to give muske to the deafe or to paynt a house for blinde men, but shall also be an endless confusion " Hewson, (1963): 30.

It appears that some of the E.E.I.C. ships sailing to the Indies were using plane charts. The journal of Captain James Burges who sailed from England to the Cape of Good Hope in the E.E.I.C. ship <u>Abegalie</u>, in August 1622 tabulates the following: day, wind, course, way, distance sailed in leagues, latitude, longitude, difference in latitude and variation. His entry for the first 3 days is interesting, having way S.W.$\frac{1}{2}$W. he sailed 84 leagues from latitude 49°50'S. to 47°10'S. and obtained his first calculated longitude of 3° west of the Lizard. Thus d.lat. = 2°40' and the departure is 195 miles W. in 47°10'S. By plane chart, his longitude would be 3°15'W., and by the Mercator chart 4°54'W., thus clearly he was using a plane chart. Not surprisingly his longitude for the Cape of Good Hope was incorrect, being 27°E. of the Lizard which is perhaps not as far out from the true value of 23°E. as one would expect (original Correspondence, (1622), Vol. 9 No. 1060). Plane charts seem to have been used by E.E.I.C. ships, but often they do not state which type of chart they were using (see above). In the E.E.I.C. fleet that sailed from the Downs on 24 March 1624, commanded by Weddell in the <u>Royal James</u> (Richard Swanley as Master, Henry Whetely as Purser), sailing with the <u>Jonas</u>, <u>Star</u> and two pinnaces <u>Spy</u> and <u>Scout</u>, we have reference to the use of 'playne' charts. The log of the <u>Royal James</u> kept by Richard Monck records as follows: "Moonth of Juley Anno Domine 1624. The 13th wee mett with weedes called Strumblowes a good signe of neerness [of the Cape of Good Hope] and then by my iudgment I was some 50 or 60 leagues of butt by reckoning I was 8 les of. The 14th wee made the Land being the Sugar loafe bareing E. by S. by Compas some 10 les of ... the longitud wee mad from the Lizard marridian to the marridian of the cape of good hope 24 degrees according to the Playne. (Raven-Hart, (1967): 88.)

13

The Nederland engraver and map-maker Jodocus Hondius brought out new editions of Mercator's work in the late 16th century. Edward Wright, the Cambridge mathematician, published in 1599 his Certaine Errors in Navigation which explained the mathematical principles of the new Mercator Projection (Wright 1599). However, the new projection which gave all places and distances the same relationship as they have on the terrestrial globe, was slow to be adopted. In 1615, John Daniel had drawn a chart of the Atlantic on the Mercator Projection for the E.E.I.C. and it was used by Row, the English commander in 1615, on his voyage to the Indies. Notwithstanding, the use of the inferior plane chart persisted well into the 18th century.

The E.E.I.C. navigators were using charts on the Mercator Projection as early as 1610 (Waters, 1958:224). An example of the use of the Mercator Projection is given in John Vian's log onboard the Discovery, homeward bound from the Persian Gulf: "Julie Anno Domine 1631. From sunn set the 11th to noon the 12th the wind at E.S.E. and S.E., Cours saild NoNoW½No leags 12 ... the Cap bonsperance bearing of me N.N.E. 4 leags of or 5 the tabell N.b E. And Chapmans Chaunce No½W, 10 leags of at noon latitud obs 34 d 30 x Longitud from the Iland Morrissis 32 d 50 xp. mercator 39 d 02 x." (Raven-Hart, 1967:106).

An interesting note on the Mercator projection was made by Thomas Bonner in 1614 on his voyage to the Indies as mate of the Expedition, (Strachan and Penrose, 1971): "25 Daye [June 1615] latti by ob 34d & 40' and longi from the Cape of Good Hope 8d &20'. This 24 houres sayled 34 leags ENE: the wind SE. This afternoone we sawe lande about some 6 leags of[f]: this lande lyes in the latti of 34 degrees and is in longi from the Cape 8d &20['] by my judgmente. This lande is layde very false in the plats that are made after Mercators projecktion: it hathe neyther true longi nor true latti, not by two degrees apeece: and betwixt the Cape of Good Hope and the baye of Augusteene it is layede 5 degrees and 20 minits shorte of the longi whiche it shoulde have: a mayne and a grosse fault: and I muche wonder it hathe not beene remedyed by such Masters and pilots as hath beene here before." Later Bonner states (7 July): "This daye at none by Mercators projecktion I am ashore: but by plano I finde my ship to be 87 leags of, a great difference, [Margin Note]: 87 leags difference in John Daniels plats, Mercator and plano and no [on?] other plats that wee have in the ship it differs 100 leags."

It is interesting to note that the Governeur-Generaal of the V.O.C. in the Indies, Jan Pieterszoon Coen, recommended corrections to the plane charts in 1627 between the Cape and the Southland. This resulted from his experience while sailing to the Indies in the Galias, in company with the Utrecht and Texel. After sailing from the Cape in latitude 37.5°S., the Galias was separated from the others. On the afternoon of the 5 September, 1627 (new style), Coen came upon Eendrachtsland, "We were at less than half a mijl's distance from the breakers before perceiving the same, without being able to see land. If we had come upon this place in the night-time, we should have been in a thousand perils with our ship and crew. In the plane charts, the reckonings of our stuerluijden were still between 300 and 350 mijlen from any land ... although the reckoning of the chart with increasing degrees showed only 120 mijlen, and the reckoning by the terrestrial globe only 50 mijlen distance from the land ... . It seems certain now that the miscalculation involved in the plane chart from Cabo de bon' Esperança to the South-land in 35 degrees latitude gives an overplus of more than 270 mijlen of sea, a matter to which most stuerluijden pay little attention ... It would be highly expedient if in the plane charts most in use, between Cabo de Bon' Esperança and the South-land south of Java, so much space were added and passed over in drawing up the reckonings, as deducable from the correct longitude according to the globosity of the earth and sea. We would request your Worships to direct attention to this point, and have such indications made in the plane chart as experts shall find to be advisable; a matter of the highest importance, which if not properly attended to involves grievous peril to ships and crews (which God in his mercy avert). In this plane chart the South-land also lies fully 40 mijlen more to eastward than it should be,which should also be rectified." Heeres, 1899:19.

In the same vein the commandeur of the ship het Wapen van Hoorn, opperkoopman J. van Roosenbergh stated in 1627: "By estimation we have got into [left blank] Longitude, ... which in the plane charts makes a considerable difference, about 217 mijlen by calculation ... it will be expedient in the plane chart to mark out a distance of about 200 mijlen, to westward of St. Paulo island and to eastward of Madagascar, the said distance to be passed over in drawing up reckonings, seeing the plane chart involves serious drawbacks; the same might well be done to eastward of the Cape, in such fashion as your Worships' cartographers and other experts, such as Master C. J. Lastman, shall find to be most expedient for the Company's service ... By estimation the land of d'Eendracht is marked in the chart fifty mijlen too far to eastward." Heeres, 1899: 20.

6. THE FIRST ENGLISH VOYAGE USING THE BROUWER ROUTE

The first E.E.I.C. ships to sail on the Brouwer Route were a fleet of three ships bound for Bantam under the command of Captain Humfry Fitzherbert in 1620. They were Fitzherbert's Royal Exchange, the Unity, and the Bear. Fitzherbert arrived at the Cape of Good Hope with the Unity on the 24 June. The ships anchored at Soldania Bay where they met up with the Surat fleet of the E.E.I.C.: Roebuck, London, Hart and Eagle under command of Captain Andrew Shilling. Also at the Cape were 9 V.O.C. ships, Hollandia, Leijden, Medenblick, Wapen van Enkhuijsen, Schoonhoven, Wapen van Hoorn, Mauritius, Ziericzee and Groeninghen, which were outward bound for Bantam under command of Nicolas van Baccum, and the E.E.I.C. ship Lyon, which was homeward bound. The Lyon and the V.O.C. fleet departed on the 25th June shortly before the arrival of another V.O.C. ship Schiedam of the Chamber of Delft which had departed from Goeree on 8 April (new style) under command of John Cornelius Kunst.

The two English commanders who had erected a camp on land were very suspicious of the Schiedam thinking she might be a pirate ship. Later, when it was discovered she belonged to the V.O.C., the commanders, it is recounted, became very friendly. It was at this time that the Cape was claimed by the English: "We notice that some [the V.O.C.] did purpose to erect a plantation in Soldania baye and that we should be frustrated of watering but by licence, whereupon our Captain intreating Captain Shilling to assist him and calling a consultation it was concluded to intitle his Majeste king supreme head and governor of that continent not yet inhabited by any Christian Prince. The same with all solemnitie by the English and Dutch was performed the 3 of July, a mount of stones being raised cald by the name of King James his Mount, and a small flag delivered to the natives which they carefully kept." Raven-Hart, 1967:71. The <u>Bear</u> arrived on 10 July, the Surat fleet departed on the 25 July and the <u>Schiedam</u> and the Bantam fleet on the 26 July. Raven-Hart, 1967:70, 73.

The skipper of the Schiedam advised Fitzherbert of the Brouwer Route: "The 26 July wee departed from Soldania Bay in companie wth. the <u>Shydam</u> of [D]elfh, Mr. Cornilious Kunst, our corse beinge to the Southward, untill wee came into $38\frac{1}{2}$ degrees, so runninge uppon a paralell about 900 leages, hopinge to fynd St. Paulo Iland, wch. by judgment was now neerupon in 38 degree where wee found great store of shoules, chandge of watter and weeds, but in regards it was neere night and much wynde, wee steered a more notherlie corse to avoyde danger... 17 Septem.: it pleased god wee made the land of Java to ye eastward of Java 150 leages (in 8 degrees and 10 mynnets) from ye Straights of Sunda." Letter from the factors aboard the <u>Royal Exchange</u> to the Company, 15 October, 1620. Original Correspondence: Vol. 7, No. 900.

The statement of finding shoals in latitude 38°S., 900 leagues east of the Cape is interesting, as by estimation this would put the vessel in longitude about 75°E. St. Paul Island lies in latitude $38^{\circ}44$'S. longitude $77^{\circ}30$'E, and Amsterdam Island in latitude $37^{\circ}50$'S. longitude $77^{\circ}30$'E. Thus it is more likely that they passed near Amsterdam Island. Also their distance estimate is remarkably accurate, (38 leagues short).

7. BUSINESS RELATING TO THE DEPARTURE OF THE TRIAL FROM PLYMOUTH

The first reference to the <u>Trial</u> in the E.E.I.C. records is in the Court of Committees held on 13 July, 1621: 'It appeered to the Court by some lres. from Mr. Boate at Plimouth that the Companies shipp the <u>Triall</u> will verry shortly be readie to putt to sea and therefore it is time to thinck upon a Maister and supply of men for that voyage. It was said that the Companie hath certanly newes by the Dutch shippes out of the Indies good or bad and therefore howsoever the shipp might be ready yet it will not be unwise to staie her untill by rading of their lres. They might know what new direcons wil be fitt to be given thether. That a Mr. wilbe fitt to be puided [?] here, but for men it was advertised from the shipp that they could be supplied wch. will save their Conduct mony." Court Book 5:7. (Unfortunately the proceedings of the E.E.I.C. Court are missing for the months between 22 March and 4 July, 1621. In this period the <u>Trial</u> must have been bought or its building and naming completed.)

There is an indirect reference to the fact that the company, "... purposeth to send out no more but one small shipp betweene this and Michas. [Michaelmas?]". Court Book 5, 8 March, 1621: 360. This is in reference to an application of Mr. Pruson to save the Company money on the design of sails, masts and cordage. There was some debate as to the skill of Mr. Pruson.

There were three ships at the time in England with the name Trial, the Triall of Aldborough, the Triall of London, and the Triall of Orston. (High Court of Admiralty Criminal Records). The Triall of London is possibly the ship involved in the abortive Virginia venture of 1606-7, and which belonged at that time to a group of citizens and fishmongers of London and was 160 tons burden, (see Quinn, 1971). The Triall of Orston is mentioned in the Exchecquer Port Book of Plymouth and Ffolley, 1619-21, 27 September 1620. "Of the Triall of Orston burtome 40 tonns, George Trigge Mr. from Bilboa" and a further entry on 26 February 1621 for the same ship this time 30 tonns. However, this ship, although located in Plymouth (Orston is on the other side of the river Plym from Plymouth), would have been an extremely small ship for such a voyage. The author is unable to find further details of the Triall of Aldborough.

A letter from Mr. Swanley in Plymouth informed the E.E.I.C. on the 19 July 1621, that the Triall would be ready for sea in 10 days. On the 20 July Mr. Newport, "... who had formly bene named to the Companie to go Mr. of the Triall cannott yett resolve whether to undertake the charge yett or not untill he have first sattisfied his wife, which he would do forthwith and then give his answeare." Court Book 5:22. The Company resolved to hold the Trial in Plymouth in the meantime until the latest letters from the Indies arrived so that the Company could then decide what needed to be sent to the Indies. Two months' wages were sent to Plymouth for the crew while the boat was idle. On the 23 July, letters were received from the Indies via a fleet of V.O.C. ships returning to Nederland. As a result it was resolved to send to the Indies in the Trial small items such as sheathing nails, hunthorns, cartridges, sheet lead.

On the 10 August, 1621: "Mr. Brookes Mr. of the Triall beeing now ready to go downe to Plimouth desired allowence for the carrying downe of himself and fouer servanntes. The Court ordered he should have 13 poundes." Court Book 5:45. By the 7 September, the Company received a letter from Mr. Bagg the younger at Plymouth, "... where in he complained exceedingly of the fienderies of the men of the Triall who over and above what the Companie had allowed did exacte two months paie but having received it and are now quieted and expect but a faire wind to begonn." Court Book 5:80. The Trial sailed from Plymouth on the 4 September: "Mr. Swanley delivered unto the Courte the State of the Companies shipp lately departed from Plimouth that she is both well manned viz 143 good men and that himself and Mr. Bagg, the elder, went out in her at their goinge awaie and made two or three boardes to trie how stiffe syded she is and found that she beare all her sailes exceedinge well wch. gave good content to the Mr. who in his lres. to Mr. Gouvrno. before he sett saile had made a question of her going by a wind." Court Book 5, 14 September 1621: 87. These are virtually all the contemporary references in England to the Trial prior to her loss.

8. THE ACCOUNT OF THE LOSS OF THE TRIAL

On 11 January 1622, the President and Council of the E.E.I.C. in the Indies wrote to the Company of their fear that the Trial and the Whale may have been lost on the backside (south coast) of Java. On the 25 June 1622, Captain John Brookes arrived at Jacatra (Batavia) in a skiff with 9 others to announce the loss of the Trial off the Great Southland.

From Brookes' letters we learn that the Trial arrived safely at the Cape of Good Hope where they encountered the returning East Indiaman Charles, under the command of Captain Bickle. Brookes asked Captain Bickle's Master mate Mr. Carter and others if they would accompany him to the Indies as neither he nor any of his mates had sailed previously from the Cape to Jacatra. Captain Bickle was willing to let any of his mates go, but none volunteered.

Brookes, departed from the Cape on 19 March and, following Fitzherbert's Journal, sailed south to latitude 39°S. and then east on that parallel.

On 1 May land was sighted in latitude 22°S.: "Wch. land had bene formlie seene by ye flemings and is sayd in ye cardes N.E. by N. and south E. by S. from Straits of Sunday. This ilande is 18 leagues long and we were all verie joyfull at ye sight thereof, but finding 8 degs, variation found by our judgment and by Capt. Fitzherberts Jornall, yt. he went 10 leagues to ye Southwardes of this iland and being in this variacon he stered N.E. by E. and fell wth. ye East end of Java." Letter of John Brookes to E.E.I.C. 25 August, 1622, Original Correspondence, Vol. 9, No. 1072.

The Trial experienced north easterly winds from the 5 May until the 24 May which prevented Brookes from heading to Java. On the 24 May: "ye great iland wth. his 3 smale ilands at ye Easten end bearing S.E. 20 leags. of us, ye winds vearing to ye S.E. and faire weather we steared N.E. thinking to falle wth. ye western pt. of Java, ye 25th daye at 11 of ye clocke in ye night, faire weather and smoth ye ship strocke, I ran to ye poope and hove ye leade and found but 3 faudoms water, 60 men being upon ye decke 5 of them would not beleave yt. she strooke. I cringe to them to beare up and tacke to ye westwards, they did ther beste, but ye rock being sharpe ye shipp was presentlie full of water, for ye most part of these rocks lie 2 fadom under watter, it strucke my men in such a mayze when I said ye shipp strooke and they could se neyther breach, land, rocks, change of watter nor signe of danger, ye shipp setting a gad while after, yet I had hove ye lead wilst I had brought my sayles a backstaies before she strooke and ? strooke, ye wind began suddenly to freshen and bloweing I strooke round my sayles and gott out my skiffe and bid them sound about ye shippe, they found sharpe suncken rockes a half a cable lenth astarne noe ground these rocks are steepe to so I made all ye waye I could to gett out my long boate and by two of ye clocke I had gotten her out and hanged her in ye tackles on ye side, soe seing ye shipp full of watter and ye winde to increase made all ye meanes I could to save my life and as manie of my compa. as I could." Original Correspondence, Vol. 9, No. 1072.

Brookes climbed down a rope out of the poop into the skiff at 300 hrs, at 400 hrs, the boat got off and at 430 hrs the fore-part of the ship broke up.

Of a total of 139, ten people, including Brookes got off in the skiff, and 36 in the long boat. Presumably 4 had died on the way out since she had departed with 143 men. The V.O.C. records state that there were 141 on board. (Heeres, 1899:13A.)

Brookes indicated that he visited the nearby islands: "My boate stood backe for ye great Iland wch. is 7 leags to ye S.E. warde of ye place where ye shipp was Cast awae ye boate found a little low Iland, these rocks and Ilands wth. there latitud, longitude, variations courses and distances I have given 2 drafts to yor. worps. psident. wch. his worps. doth intend to send you ye first conveyance, I fell wth. ye Easter end of Java ye 8th daie of June, 1622." (Original Correspondence, Vol. 9, No. 1072.) There are several references to Brookes' charts being sent home but unfortunately they appear to have been subsequently lost. Brookes in the skiff had one barrecoe (a Barrico - keg: (Onions, 1968)) of water, 2 cases of bottles, 2 runlets (large runlets varied between 54 and 83 dm^3, small runlets between 14 and 18 dm^3: (Onions, 1968)) of aquivite, 4 lbs (?) bread. The boat with Bright had 22 runlets of wine, 6 barrecoes of water, 2 cases of bottles and 4 lbs bread.

9. BROOKES' RESPONSIBILITY: ERROR OR FALSIFICATION?

There can be little doubt of the validity of Lee's identification of Ritchie Reef as the rocks on which the Trial was lost (see Introduction).

Brookes mentions an island in lat. 22°S. about 18 leagues long; this is almost certainly the coast between N.W. Cape and Pt Cloats, which from the N.W. appears as an island. Brookes' description of 3 small islands off the eastern end of this great island, corresponds with the small islands off N.W. Cape. From a position 20 leagues N.W. of N.W. Cape, Brookes then sailed N.E. The next day on a course N.E. and N.E. by E., the Trial was wrecked. This course passes quite close to Trial Rocks, and would be within a day's sailing of it. The subsequent description of islands, shoals, and a great island to the S.E. by both Brookes and Bright, can be identified as present-day Monte Bello Islands and Barrow Island (fig. 4).

Brookes obviously falsified the evidence to maintain the fiction that he was following Fitzherbert's Journal, as instructed by the E.E.I.C. He had to state that he, like Fitzherbert, sailed in a north-easterly direction; thus he could claim that Fitzherbert narrowly missed the same rocks, and so establish that he (Brookes) was in no way to blame for the disaster.

He pretended that initially he had thought the Straits lay N.E. by N. of the wreck's position, but after making the eastern end of Java on a N.E. by N. course, he corrected his position to allow for this, putting the position of Trial Rocks 200 leagues further to the east, due south of the Straits of Sunda.

For Brookes to have made a landfall after the wreck on the eastern end of Java, he must have sailed due north from Trial Rocks. Even if he had made a serious mistake in calculating his longitude, this landfall would have indicated the error. If he had continued on a N.E. course from Trial Rocks he would have passed east of Timor.

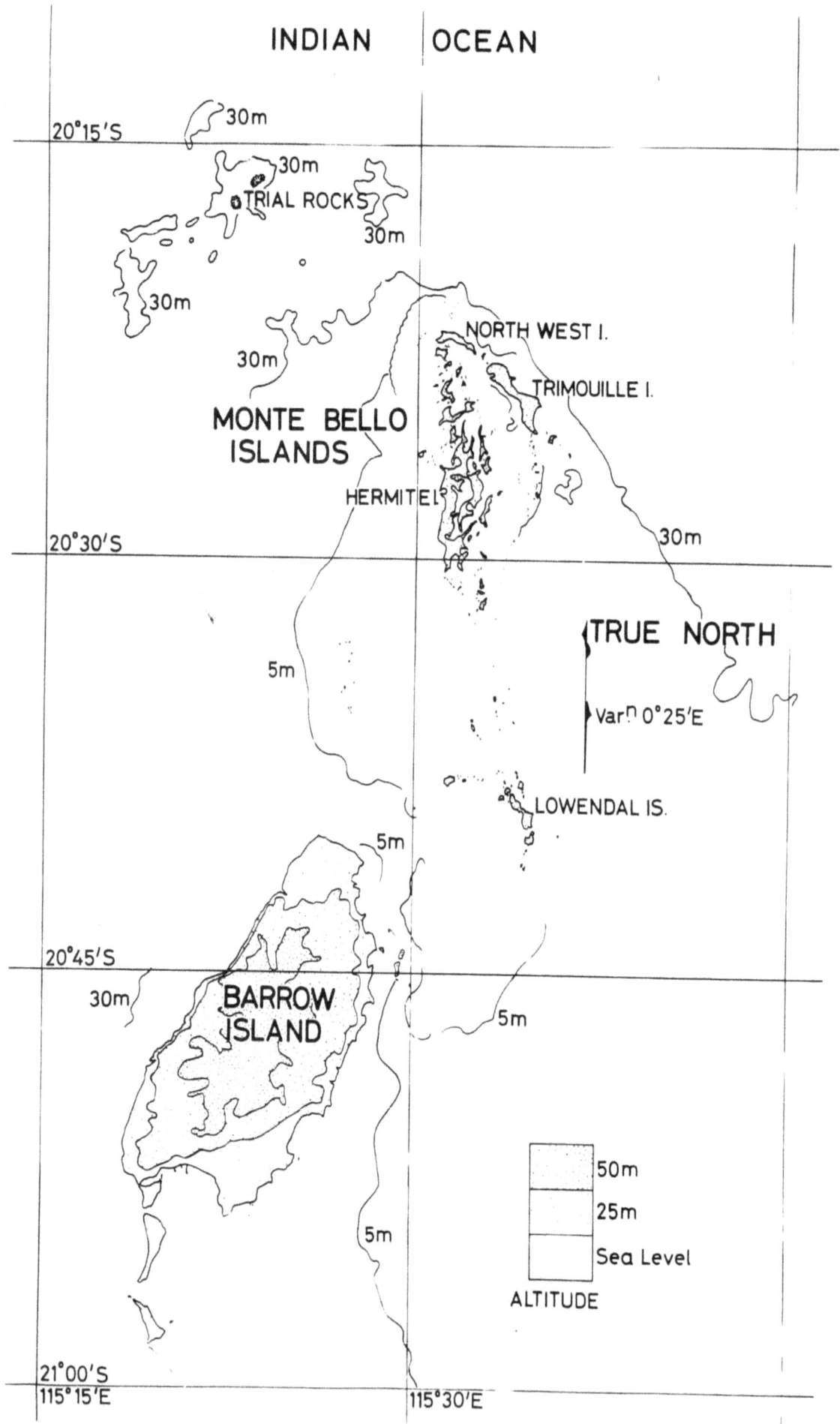

Fig. 4   Chart of Trial Rocks, Monte Bello Islands and Barrow Island, taken
from Admiralty Chart.

Brookes' story is completely consistent, but entirely false. Duped by the elaborate lie, the E.E.I.C. never imputed to Brookes any culpability for the loss of the Trial. However, a witness to the events, the Trial's factor Thomas Bright believed Brookes was guilty of negligence, and held him responsible for the catastrophe. In a letter to one Andrew Ellam, Bright gives his account of the loss of the Trial. "May ye 25th about X of clock night, fayre weather and little wind in Lattitud 20°3' and Longitude 80° nerest, 300 leagues from the Straights of Sundaye shipp Tryall, by Carelessnes for want of looking out, struck upon the rocks ...... his crew [Brookes'] and fellowe and consorts providing provisions and safeing his things, bearing Mr. Jackson and myselfe wth. fayre words promising us faythfully to take us along, butt like a Judasse turning my back into greatt cabbin lowerd himself privattly into the skiffe, only wth. 9 men, and his boye, stood for the Straights of Sunday that instant, wth. out care and seeinge the lamentable end of shipp the tyme shee splitt or respect of any mans life, the long boate wth. great difficultie wee gott out being 128 soules left to gods mercy ..... wee keeping till day some ¼ mile from the shipp, then findinge rocks in many places, the sea then so high wee durst not for feare of indaingering ourselves adventur to them and for thatt wee so slenderly provided wth. provisions ..... uppon sight of day wee espied a iland bearing south East some five leagues att most from us [North West Island] by all likelyhoode land could not be far by the fowle and weede all that day drivinge from the iland to wch. said iland wee went stayed theron seaven [days?] ...... not any inhabitants theron, wee travelled on all the iland seeing nothing but ilands some small some greatt breaches and shoules every way as farr as wee could see [the Monte Bello Group] very daingerous on the N.W. syde to the S.S.W. of this Ile ther lyeth a greatt Iland neere nyne leags off [Barrow Island]. The full descripcon of these Ilands I would have sent you butt many things I want to laye them downe truly as I could wish, reffer yor. to presse of tyme this from mee how [?]. I am not one that posesse marriners Art or any skill therin worth the notting yett this much I understand by relacon of Jornalls and platts that these Ilands weer never discovered by any, ... June the iith steered for the place we left our shipp, sayling betwixt the Breches had 20 fathom, nothing wee could see of shipp or any thing aptaying therto." Bright's letter gives further evidence of Brookes' falsification: "... [Brookes] would excuse itt [the loss] to say he followed directly captin Humphrie Fitz Harbotte Jornall, had our Jornalls bin compared wth. his he should have found Broocks 400 leagues in the Lattitud of 38° to 34° more to the Eastward then he or ever shippe was againe, wee allwayes feared the shipp to be beyound his recknoing (well nigh uppon 380 leagues [crossed out]), the wind that present wee, strucke S.S.E. he directing his Course north East and north East and be East, when the Straights of Sunday bore north westerly of us." This letter was dated at Jacarta, 22 August 1622, about a month after Bright's arrival. It is possible that Bright was aware of Brookes' error (that the Straits of Sunda lay N.W.) at the time of the loss, but he must have been certain of Brookes' falsification after his own landfall on Java and after Brookes' claim that Trial Rocks lay S. of the Straits. Bright accused Brookes in his letter of various other crimes including theft: " ... itt dyd seeme straing to mee that Broocks had so Cunningly Excused, the, neglect of the Comps. lers. spangls and monys, ye monys he Confessed to the president and Mr. Brokenden to have Cfer. of mee, he for a matter nigh 2 howers, nothing butt convaying from his Cabin to his [Chest (crossed out)]. Skiffe to my knowledge both lers. monys, spangls were layd in his trunke, wherof many of thes things, apparell and other trifels, he have by him this present, & report of of [sic] his matts. that came a long with him in the skiffe the Black Box wherin the Companys lers. weere weer [sic] seen, presently after they left the shippe also & his owne Confesion, lers. my self Conveyed into the skiffe, somefor the Presidnt and somefor Mr. Brokendon, and others were heaved over bord his excuse hereing; answering they weer wett, and yett not so wett butt he pused the Contents therof, wch. he well knew would have donne him noe good, if he had honestly delivered them." Original Correspondence, 22 August 1622, Vol. 9, No. 1070. This letter which is noted on the first page to Andrew Ellam is unsigned; the last page or pages together with the envelope and delivery notes are missing. Sainsbury suggested that the writer was Bright, the grounds for this identification being that Bright was in charge of the longboat (Sainsbury, 1970:134). The Table of Contents of Volume 9 of the Original Correspondence gives no author, but was probably compiled when the volumes were bound at a much later date than the correspondence.

10. THE SUBSEQUENT CAREER OF CAPTAIN JOHN BROOKES IN THE INDIES

The President and Council of the E.E.I.C. wrote to the Company at home soon after the arrival of Brookes, "... therefore wee have deleyned hime here, not knowinge what wants your shippes abroade may have of such men." Original Correspondence, 27 August 1622. Vol. 9, No. 1076.

Meanwhile, the President and Council sent Brookes on a voyage of exploration around Sumatra, in the ship Little Rose. Brookes noted in a letter to the Company in England, 10 December 1623: "... the river of Chamysoare, upon Sumatra, & great Bessee are very good places, but for Sabacoare I doe not lyke it so well. I hope my draughts & remembrances of these places, delivered to the President & his Councell will give yr. worps. great content." Brookes continues: "Also the President & Councell have made mee Captain Robart Addams his successour, Comannder of the Shippe Moone of wch. I hope by gods helpe to make a suffitient shipp to goe home in November next according to the President & Councell pmise., and wthall. the President hath pmised. to goe home in her himselfe, wch. causes mee soe willingly to stay, & wthall. to save soe worthy a shipp. It was made a great wonder to careene a great shipp at Hectores Iland before I undertooke it, & careened the Exchange to the keele, the Anne haulfe a carreene, the Rose & Unitie each a whole carreene. I hope god will give a blessinge to the Moone to a whole careene, wch. I make noe doubt of if there bee noe worse matter then as yet it to bee pceaved. howsoever indevour shall not bee wantinge. If shee should not goe home the next yeare then shee is a shipp lost, if shee had gone home in the Paulsgraves roome, shee had bene very sufficient & noe doubt but to have gone as well home as the Paulsgrave I hope is & I doubt not but the next yeare the Moone will bee at home." Original Correspondence, Vol. 10 No. 1127.

The Moone, Discovery and Ruby set sail from Lagundy Island, a new and unsuccessful E.E.I.C. post in the Straits of Sunda, on 15 February, 1625. President Brockendon, who was travelling with them, died on the voyage and was buried at the Cape.

The Moone had first gone to the Indies in 1618, and had seen considerable service there. In 1619 she was part of the fleet which fought a battle with the V.O.C. fleet near Jacatra, in which over 1000 shot were fired from each fleet in less than 3 hours. (Original Correspondence, 23 February, 1619. Vol. 6, No. 759.) The Moone was then dispatched to Engano with the Clove, Globe, Peppercorn, Advice and Dragon's Claw, to recover goods from an E.E.I.C. wreck (the Sun).

In July 1620, with the Paulsgrave and the rest of the Manila fleet, she departed for Japan, where a mutiny took place. After this was resolved, the Moone did various voyages for the Company in the Indies.

In a letter dated 3 August 1625 from Henrie Hawley and others to the E.E.I.C., it was noted that the English ships in the Indies were so weakened by desertions and unexpected disasters, that when the Moone, Ruby, and Discovery were to be manned for the homeward voyage, the Hart for Macassar and the Coaster for Jambi, the Charles, Bull, Reformation, Roebuck, Diamond, Abigail and Rose were hardly able to man a boat to fetch their water. Original Correspondence: Vol. 11, No. 1203. Thus, in February 1625, the Moone left the Indies for the last time.

11. THE LOSS OF THE MOONE

"On Satterday agoe a fortnight in the morning hee [Mr. Governor] had news brought to him of the arrivall of 4 of their shipps from the East Indies and also of a fift shippe wch. was unfortunately Cast away upon our Coast." Thus the Court of Committees of the E.E.I.C. in London recorded the news of the loss of the Moone, (Court Book 8, 4 October, 1625: 116117). Serious charges of negligence and wilfully casting away of the Moone were laid against Brookes and the master, Churchman. Both men were imprisoned in Dover Castle. In December 1625, Brookes started to petition from Dover Castle to come to trial.

The Company examined Thomas Saunderson, the purser of the Diamond, (one of the fleet of ships that returned from the Indies with the Moone). "Saunderson was willed to relate unto them what words he had heard Captaine Brookes speake concerning the shipp Moone, who made answeare that he heard him say at the Cape [of Good Hope] that he would turn the Nose of the shippe the wrong way and to that he would be deposed, As allso that he wished that the said shipp were at Ligorne", (a famous pirate entrepot). Court Book 8:140.

Brookes answered this charge in a long statement read to the Court on 19 April, 1626: "John Brookes late Mr. of the Moone preted himselfe this day to the Court, desired theire favor, that he might be permitted to answeare those caluminced, and fallse accusacons wch. he understands are imposed uppon him, as being the cheife and only cause in casteing away the said Shippe the Moone, neere Dover roade, pretending he shall be able soe to cleere himselfe .... where uppon Brookes pulling a paper out of his pockett begann to declare, that this unfortunate accident, had murthered him of his reputacon and robbed him of his meanes and from thence fell to relate pticculary and by way of Journall, his Journey to the Indies in 1622, and the manner how theire shippe the Tryall, whereof he was then Mr. was cast away, still ex-cuseing himselfe not to be faulty therein, but that it might have bynn the most skillfull Mariners mishappe, that is best accquainted wth. those seas to have had the like disaster, insisting much uppon his care and direction of Captaine Ffitzherberts Journall wch. he punctually followed ...., he further alleadged that beeing prest to take his Voyage homeward in the Moone, he absolutely refused to undertake the same knowing her weakned, and how extreamely she was eaten wth. the wormes, but at the incouragmt. of Mr. Brockenden he altered his resolucon, in regard the said Mr. Brockenden promised to venter him-selfe in the said Shippe. He accused Saunders, as the ground and mayne of this scandall raised uppon him, adding Scudamore and Hunter as confederates in giveing out that he would runn away wth. the shippe, to which he gave this answeare, that beeing at the Cape and findeing her very leake, he confessed he used theise words, that he wished the shippe in a safe harbor. and named Ligorne, shewing further his intention, when he came in to the Sleeve, to have put into the Isle of Wight, but by tempest was driven into the Nesse by Wight, and then prepared himself to come into the Downes, afirmeing that when the shippe strucke aground he was not prst. at the openinge of Mr. Brockendens Chest nor had any of the diamonds or jewells, but confessed his boy had them, for when he came ashoare, Mr. Yonge searched him to the skynne, who found nothing of him, but a paire of lynen breeches, heeruppon he inveighed against Mr. Yonge, for causeing him to be comitted, and com-playned against the Company for keepeing of him in prison seaven monthes wthout. calling him to answeare, there haveing beene 14 Courts of Admiralltie in that tyme. .... Mr. Deputy then demanded of him what he did further desire, for whatsoever he had deliverred, was rather a repeticon of his life, then any manifestacon or cleereing of his inocency, his request was to come to a speedie tryall." Court Book 8: 369-371. The Court agreed to proceed as quickly as possible in this matter. On the 21 April 1626, Brookes made a curious request to the Committee, "... on the behalfe of his sonne, not only for the payment of his wages but for such monneyes as he deliveared into the Companies Cashe in the Indies and is expressed in the Pursers bookes, being a matter of X £ [£10]. The Court called for the boy in, and after many questions demannded of him concerning the casting away of the said Shippe, and whether his father was not an Actr. and present at the breakeing upp of Mr. Brockendens Chest, and who had his jewells, and diamonds, and such like, to wch. the Boy most cautiously and cunningly answeared, and in all excused his father, but accused Churchman the Mr., Stamper the Boatswayne and himself. Churchman to have taken the Bezar stonnes and himself the Diamonds, wch. were afterwards taken away from him by Mr. Yonge. The Court having thus questioned him and haveing noe exception against him, was pleased in favo, the boy to give order for payment of the said X£ [£10] and such wages as are due unto him for the time of his being in the Country." Court Book 8: 375-376. It seems quite extraordinary that someone caught stealing diamonds from the chest of the late Governor of the Company in the Indies should still be paid his wages.

Finally, on 1 May 1626, John Brookes petitioned the House of Commons in a bid to bring his case to some conclusion: "The humble petition of John Brookes late commander of the shippe called the Moone belonginge to the East India Company.

"In all humble showing on ye 15th of September last thorow ye violence of the weather the fouleness of the said ship and rottenes of the sailes and ground tackel, your petitionar suffered shipwrack in the said ship for that all ordinarie menes being used, the materialls failing, the ship was cast away. Your petitioner losing his hole estate therein, only save what the company owes him not saving more than a ring on his finger and such clothes as wch. swimming he reovered to dover havace [?] of his life, whereupon save false allegations he was remaynded by the Mayer, a member of the Company to the Baylifse prison and there remayned 7 days and then was brought upp to the Castle were he continued above 6 months without being called or suffered to come to heering albeit there was in the time att leaste 12 Admirality Courts holden there and on time two Committees of the East India Company in Court and so should still have remained but uppon his petition to the Duke of Buckingham he was pleased to give warrent for his releasement, putting in surities to appear in the Castle Court att Dover." Colonial East India Papers, 1626, 4:77. In his petition to the House of Commons, Brookes claimed that he had been forced into a £1500 bond to appear in court 14 days after notification, and that the Company had done this to keep him from sea-service. In a bitter attack on the E.E.I.C., Brookes held that the Company itself was to blame for its increasing losses, by death and desertion, of seamen - a matter which greatly concerned the Company at that time.

"1. They draw them in by promising them great means.

2. When in the country [Indies] they keep them there so long, that many die for want of food and necessaries, and some run to the Portugals and the heathern so that a great many never return.

3. The sailors have but 2-3 meals of flesh a week, short measure, 2 of butter 4 ozs to 5 men, a quart of arrack in the morning to 5 men and all week else rise and water, many times short, by which the ill air many fall.

4. The Company keeps their ships so long to take purchase [to great value] from the Portugals and Chinamen, that they become so decayed that none would venture home in them but such as would rather put themselves at the mercy of god than peril in the country. Though kept labouring at the pumps all the way home and if any extreme weather happened they had small hope of safety." (Sainsbury, 1870:314).

Another interesting document relating to this case is Brookes' gunner and seaman's certificate which was more than likely used in the proceedings, it stated: "To all to whome these note shall com wee whose names are under written do testifie that ye bearar: hearof John Brooke is an abell and suffesient Gunnar for sae [sea?] or shoar and allso an [crossed out] antient [in a different hand] Seaman." Dom. Chas. I., 27 November 1626, 40:31.

The proceedings dragged on until July 1626. The E.E.I.C. petitioned the House of Lords, and the Lord High Admiral, the Duke of Buckingham. Problems were brought up about procedure, since the case came under the jurisdiction of the Cinque Ports, yet the trial was to be in the Admiralty Court.

Finally, almost in desperation, the Company decided that Brookes and Churchman could both make submissive petitions so that the whole matter could be resolved outside the Court of Law. On the 14 July 1626, the Court of Committees recorded: "The next busines was that of Brookes & Churchman whose peticon being read, wch. the court expected to have been an absolute submission, contrary wise it proved a justification of themselve, laid impitacons of injury up on the Company, demanded reparacon and seemed to desire an end, but submitted not, this peticion gave much distast to the Court, and therefore to free themselves of such clamorous petition and of the imputacons therein suggested, the Court resolved to tell them for an answere, that as they began legally so they would end legally ... and told them so much adding hosoever they insist upon. instificacon [?] yett the shippe was beastly lost." Court Book 9: 33-34.

At times the proceedings seem more like a Gilbert and Sullivan musical comedy than a serious legal case. Brookes and Churchman accused each other of various crimes, and attacked the Company. Both men made several submissions to the Company which were unacceptable. Thus the case dragged on, to the acute embarrassment of the Company.

Finally on 4 August 1626, Brookes made a submissive petition to the Company praying their pardon. The Governor wanted an end to the proceedings as by now Brookes had no estate. The case was again referred to Sir Henry Marten's arbitration. On the 18 August 1626, Brookes and Churchman were released from the Company and all suits against them over the casting away of the Moone and Trial were dropped. (Court Book 9: 83.)

However the Company had other problems, it had previously contracted Jacob Johnson, a diver of Dover to recover the ordinance from the Moone. On the 24 July 1626 it was recorded that he had "taken upp 43 of them for wch. hee demande money whereas by bargaine he should have taken 59 that were to be seen at very low water and was not to have his money untill all were recovered... the Court wondered that in so long tyme no more were recovered especially all that were seen and conceive that he has wronged the Comp. wther. by neglecting to take them upp or by taking them upp and selling them away." Court Book 8:51. In December 1626, this question was finally resolved, and the whole matter which had been bitter and embarrassing for the Company could at last be dropped.

Once again Brookes appears as a very devious person; he was again accused of lying, theft, and incompetence. It is hard to see Brookes in anything but an unfavourable light; the events related to the loss of the Moone reflect on his involvement in the previous loss of the Trial, and the honesty of his statements related to that loss. At the same time the Company appears as a rather inefficient organization, imprisoning Brookes and Churchman, but failing to bring them to trial. The loss was serious for the company since by 1626 only about £5000 out of £55000 of the original cargo of the Moone had been recovered, much of it having been stolen, a matter of great regret to the Company, as a year after the loss they were still trying to locate the stolen pepper.

12. THE SEARCH FOR TRIAL ROCKS

The loss of the Trial caused some concern for the safety of ships sailing on the Brouwer Route to the Indies, both for the E.E.I.C. and the V.O.C. The Governor of the E.E.I.C. in the Indies wrote to the Company on 27 August 1622: "Whereas formerly wee are of oppinione that Capt. Ffitzharberts Journall of his voyage from England hither was the surest Course to get a speedie passadge from the Cape to this place doee nowe Recante from our saide oppinnone and Referre itt Unto yor. worsp. to sett a more appreond [?] Course for your shippes to followe.

"The Dutch intend allsoe to write theire maisters att home to send noe more of theire shippes soo Sowtherly a course for some of theire shippes have nowe lately escaped verry narrowly uppon the Sowth maine Contynent, which you may please to take noatins of, and Reforme your seas Carde, accordinge to the draught wich wee send you preeveously from Mr. Brookes." Original Correspondence, Vol. 9, No. 1076.

Brookes advised the company: "... not anie shipp should passe 37 degs. and so to rune 1000 leagues in tht. paralell from thence to steeare rig. ye Straights of Sundaye, let anie man prsume upon yt. when he finde 10 degs. variacion having runne 1300 leagues being in ye latitude of 18 or 19 long. 74 or 75 ye Straights of Sunday will beare of him N.N.E. Ye currant setts strong to ye Eastwarde all waies in yt Course experience of variat. is ye greatest helpe to anie man." Brookes was recommending a more northerly course than the V.O.C. seijlaesorder. He also mentioned that the Wapen van Hoorn and two other ships (Amsterdam and Dordrecht) got into difficulties by sailing in latitude 42°, "this remote passidge ye Dutch generall doth not like."

This concern was underlined by a letter dated 6 September, 1622 (new style), from the Gouverneur Generaal and Raad of the V.O.C. in the Indies to the Company at home: "On the 5th of July [new style] there arrived here [Batavia] a skiff with ten men forming part of the crew of an English ship, named the Trial, and on the 8th do. her boat with 36 men. They state they have lost and abandoned their ship with 97 men and the cargo she had taken in, on certain rocks situated in Latitude 20°10' South, in the longitude of the western extremity of Java. These rocks are near a number of broken islands, lying very wide and broad, S. East and N. West, lying at 30 mijlen N.N.E. of a certain island, which in our charts is laid down in 22°S. Lat. ... The ship 't Wapen van Hoorn has also been in extreme peril: at night in a hard wind she got so near the land d'Eendracht or the Southland of Java that she was in 6 fathom before they saw land, which they could noways put off from, so that they ran on it. But shortly after the storm abating, they got the landwind, and came off safe for which the Lord be praised.

"The ships Amsterdam and Dordrecht likewise got into great peril near the land just mentioned in the year 1619. Where as it is necessary that ships, in order to hasten their arrival, should run on an eastward course for about 1000 mijlen from the Cape de Bona Esperance between 40 and 30 degrees Southern Latitude, it is equally necessary that great caution should be used and the best measures taken in order to avoid such accidents as befell the English ship Trial. They say that they met with this accident through following the course of our ships; that they intend to dissuade their countrymen from imitating their example, and that their masters are sure to take other measures accordingly." Heeres (1899).

The first search for Trial Rocks was proposed by the V.O.C. in the Indies as part of a general voyage of exploration of the west coast of the Southland in 1622. Instructions for this voyage were given to the jachten Haringh and Hasewint on 29 September 1622 (new style), but then the expedition was cancelled. The instructions referred to Trial Rocks: "Inasmuch as d'Heeren Majores ernestly enjoin us to dispatch hence certain jachten for the purpose of making discovery of the Zuyderlant; and ... experience has taught, by great perils incurred by sundry of our ships - but specially by the late mis-carrying of the English ship Triall on the said coast -, the urgent necessity of obtaining full and accurate knowledge of the true bearing and conformation of the said land, that further accidents may henceforth be prevented as much as possible; besides this, seeing that is highly desirable ... to ascertain whether the regions or any part of the same are inhabited, and whether any trade might with them be established, so that is why ... we have resolved to fit out the jachten Haringh and Hasewint for under taking the said voyage and for ascertaining as much of the situation and nature of these regions as God Almighty shall vouchsafe to allow them.

"You will accordingly set sail from here together, run out of Sunda Strait, and steer your course for the Suijderlant, from the western extremity of Java, keeping as close to the wind as you will find at all possible, that by so doing you may avoid being driven too far westward by the South-easterly winds which generally blow in those waters ... In running over to the Suijderland aforesaid, you will have to keep a careful lookout, as soon as you get in 14 or 15 degrees, seeing that the English ship Trial before mentioned got aground in 20°10' Southern Latitude on certain sunken rocks, bearing north-east and south-west for a length of 7 mijlen, according to the observations of the English pilot, but without having seen any mainland thereabouts. But the men who saved themselves in the schuijt and boot, and thus arrived here, deposed that in the latitude of 13 or 14 degrees they had seen sundry pieces of wood and cane, and branches of trees floating about, from which they concluded that there must be land or islands near there. The sunken rocks aforesaid on which the Trial was wrecked, were exactly south of the western extremity of Java ac-cording to the statements made by the English sailors." Heeres, 1899: 13B.

In 1636 the Gouverneur Generaal and Raad in the Indies again gave instruct-ions for an expedition to look out for Trial Rocks.

Gerrit Tomaszoon Pool was the Commandeur of the fleet of two jachten Cleen Amsterdam and Wesel, destined to depart from Banda to discover lands situated east of Banda and further of the Zuijderlandt extending to the South-West. "... and if your jachten are proof against the rough seas that prevail in the Southern Ocean in 33 and 34 degrees; after which you will return to Batavia through the Sunda Straits, trying in passing to touch at the Trials, that further information about this rock and its situation may in this way be obtained." Heeres, 1899: 25.

13. CHARTS AND EARLY ACCOUNTS OF TRIAL ROCKS

The earliest charts showing Trial Rocks were made by Hessel Gerritsz and showed Eendrachtsland and the Indies, (dated 1627 and 1618, with additions to 1628, see Schilder, 1976). Gerritsz. was the official kaartenmaker of the V.O.C. and had at his disposal the journals and documents referring to these early discoveries. The 1627 chart (fig. 5) shows Trial Rocks with the following note: "Hier ist Engels schip de Trial vergaen in Iunis Ao. 1622." (at a distance 85 mijlen slightly N. of W. by N. from the northern end of Eendrachtsland in latitude 20°10' S.). The 1628 chart (fig. 6) shows Trial Rocks 85 mijlen W.N.W. of the same point. This chart shows the relationship between the rocks and Java, Trial Rocks being marked 30 mijlen E. of the meridian of Java Head, and the Northern end of Eendrachtsland 90 mijlen E. of the same. This then shows Eendrachtsland 45 mijlen to the W. of its true position, and it remained thus on the charts until the 18th century.

Trial Rocks also appeared in the meridian of Java Head on the charts of G. Blaeu (dated 1635), and in subsequent charts of his son J. Blaeu up to 1664. The cartographer J. Hondius placed Trial Rocks in the same position on his Mercator projection chart of the Indies published in 1638. Most 17th century map and chart makers showed the rocks in this position. Notable is the chart of Sir Robert Dudley, published in his Arcano del Mare (fig.7), the first sea atlas to be published entirely on the Mercator Projection, (1646). Dudley indicated a large island and a group of rocks in between lat. 20-22°S, long. 132-137° E. of Isola de Pico in the Azores, (Carta particolare del mare d'India sino allo stretto di Sunda fra l'Isole di Sumatra e di Iava maggre con altre Isolette e scogls scop. d'Inglesi. d'Asia Carta III. (Dudley, 1661). The islands lie N.E. by S.W., the N.W. group of islands lying exactly in the meridian of Java Head and marked "Scogli doue supersa la nave Inglese di Tugall [sic]", the S.W. island is marked: "I. Scoperua da Inglesi". Dudley shows the large S.W. island 30 leagues long and the southern end of the group of islands to the N.N.E. at a distance of 40 leagues. The N.W. group of islands is 30 leagues long. It seems possible that Dudley may have seen a copy of Brookes' charts since he shows the islands (which at that time had been seen only by the survivors of the Trial) in much more detail than did other charts of the time. In view of the distance between the S.W. island and the N.W. group of islands, and the size of the former, it seems likely that the former is Eendrachtsland between the N.W. Cape and Point Cloates, and not present-day Barrow Island, an error which Brookes seems to have introduced in his letter.

Curiously, in the map of the Indian Ocean published by Valentyne (1726), "Tabula Indiaë Orientalis et Regnorum Adjacentum" by J. van Braam, Trials Rosten are shown in 19°30' S., 127°E. of Tenerif; this puts the rocks 5°E. of Java Head in long. 110°E of Greenwich. This is a curiously different position than is generally shown in 18th century maps, in this case the rocks are below the centre of Java, but still too far to the west. It should also be noted that there is in this map complete confusion over the position of the Cocos and Christmas Islands. Cocos Islands are marked near to Moni Island, possibly North Keeling. To the east is marked Christina Island and Zelan, the latter possibly being a double sighting of Christmas Island.

By the late 18th century, there was possibly even more confusion about the position of Trial Rocks than when Dudley published his Arcano del Mare in 1646. In Samuel Dunn's "A New Directory of the East Indies" (1780), Chapter CCLXXI, the "Directions for the Straits of Sunda" give the following instructions:

"A ship being off the Island of St. Paul and Amsterdam, or near them, in variation 19°W. or variation 20° W. and bound to China, through the Straits of Sunda, is not under the Necessity of making the Coast of New Holland, or running so far to the eastward; but may run 10° or 11° farther to the eastward in the latitude 37°30' S. or latitude 38°S. Having made 10° or 11° easting from St. Paul's, and in the above latitude, you may then edge away to the northward, and will then decrease your variation pretty fast. In latitude 34°46'S. and longitude made from St. Paul's 13°26'E. or hereabout, you will meet the SE. trade winds, strong gales; and in latitude 10°S. longitude made from St. Paul's 33°E. you will have variation 2°30'W. With this variation you will make land in latitude 8°16'S. 20 or 25 leagues to the eastward of Java Head; and all ships, bound through the Straits of Sunda, should take care to fall in with the land to the eastward of Java Head. Ships, for want of proper attention to the variation, have fallen in to the westward of the Straits of Sunda, and have been obliged to go through the Straits of Malacca, with great loss of time."

Chapter CCLXXIV: "Directions for sailing toward China through the Straits of Sunda, Banca, etc": "... When you are in latitude 37°S. you must keep therein, steering east, for about 1100 leagues, or till you have made about 70° east longitude from the Cape of Good Hope. It will not be absolutly necessary to see the island of St. Paul or Amsterdam, though the sight thereof will greatly assist you in rectifying your account, and shaping your course afterward. They are situated 56°30' to the eastward of this Cape, (actually 59°). The former is the northermost, and may be plainly seen 12 leagues at sea... The observations of several navigators, compared together, fix its latitude in 37°50'S.

"About 6 leagues to the southward of this lies the Island of St. Paul, which is smaller than that of Amsterdam. The variation there was observed 18°30'W. on board the Defence and other ships in 1742....

"From the Tropic of Capricorn steer NNE. to go 60 leages to the westward of Trial Rocks, which are a cluster of various high rocks above and under water, extending about 15 leagues from the east to west, and 5 leagues from the north to south. These were discovered by a Dutch ship in 1719: their existence was afterward confirmed by a sloop sent from Batavia to determine the exact situation, which was found in latitude 19°30'S. and 80 leagues west of New Holland. It will be most prudent to pass their latitude in the day-time, because you may fall foul of them at night, when you reckon yourself a good way off.

"In latitude 22°6'S. and 74°30'E. of the Cape of Good Hope, lies Cloate's Island.

"The first account we have of this is from Mr. Nash, of the ship House of Austria, from Ostend for China in 1719. They saw it first (being very clear

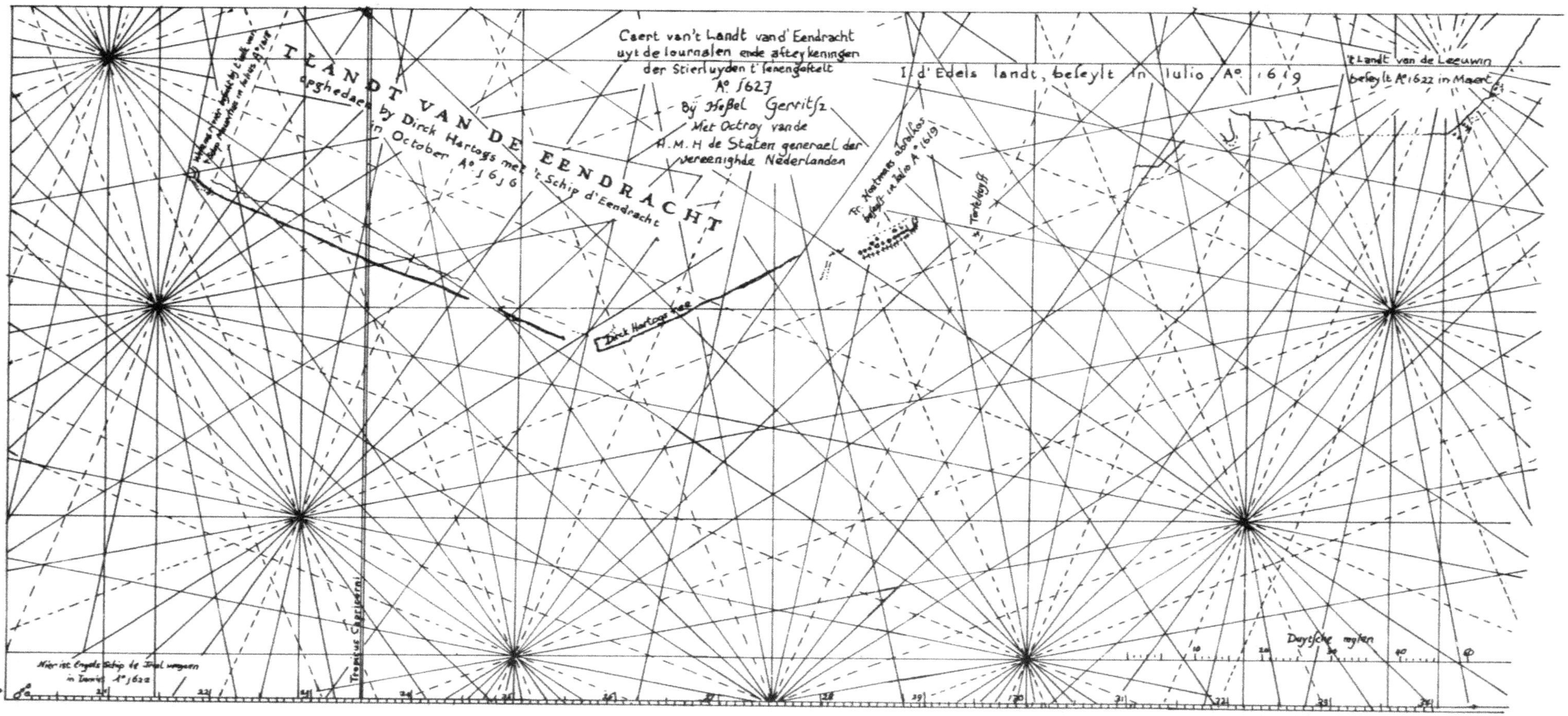

Fig. 5   Hessel Gerritsz chart of Eendrachtsland dated 1627.

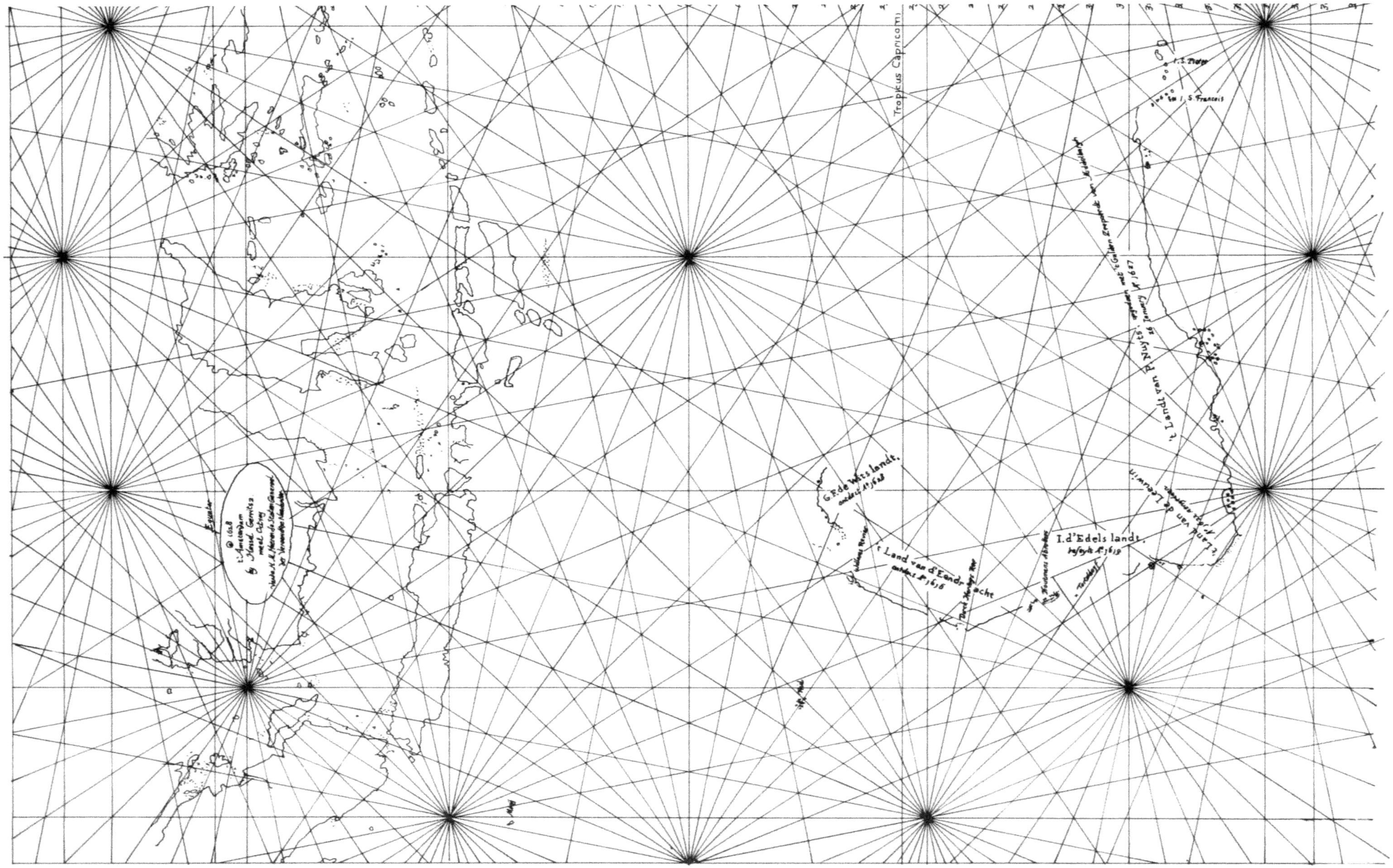

Fig. 6

Chart of Malay Archipelago and
Eendrachtsland by Hessel Gerritsz dated 1618 but with additions
to 1628.

Equinoziale'

Var. 6. Gr. t. Maestrale'

Nanaw
Anabangyoe
C. di Camfor
Palo Minoas
Prome
Tercoa
Nualam ò.
George Ernums Island
Alare S. di Nassaw

Silabom
Priaman
Sabem
Sadagara
Pom
I Sumatra
Bantopas
Bancalo
Salabar
Browns.
Sland
Salabar
Pulo Pasarom
Palembon
Sunda Camp

A da

Il Vento e'spesso per Aus-
tro uerso Libeccio

Ingano
Var. 6. Gr.
Maestrale'
Stretto di Sunda

I. Higon
Iaua Maggiore

Apoluara

Rising Iland

I Triangolare'
Scoperto' dall' Inglese

Var. g. Gr. Maestr.

L'OCEANO ORIENTALE

Scogli doue si persa
la Naue Inglese' di
Trigani
I Scopertos' Inglese

L'Venti Per Sirocco.

R. Lucius Pere

Fig. 7   Detail of Carta III from Dudley's Arcano del Mare showing Trial
Rocks, Northwest Cape and Straits of Sunda.

weather) about 3 A.M. on which they immediatly brought to and sounded, but had no ground with 100 fathoms, though not above 4 miles from shore, (some accounts say, they had no ground within 2 miles of the island)... This island cannot be seen far even in clear weather, and lies NEbN and SWbS about 32 leagues [sic] in length, with terrible breakers from each end running about 3 miles into the sea. It lies in latitude 22°S. and 92°E. longitude from the Cape. From hence they made 3°6' easting to the island of Bally [Bali] and 7°26' westing to Java Head. As they did not find account of it in their books or charts, they gave it the name of Cloate's Island, in honour of a Flemish Baron, probably one of their owners.

"The Haesingfield fell in with it in 1743 they saw it at day-light bearing SE½S. to EbS. about 6 leagues. They report it lies NE. and SW. 7 or 8 leagues in length, of a moderate height, and pretty level, with a gradual slope to each end, from whence they saw the breakers. By their accounts, they make it in latitude 22°7'S. and longitude 32°49'E. from the Island of St. Paul, and in 84°26'E. longitude from Cape Lagullas, their variation the morning before, was 6°17'N. westerly. From this island they steered nearly North for 7 days; then they made the land of Java, in latitude 8½° and 44'W. meridian distance and in 3½ days more made Java Head, in 7°12'W. longitude Cloate's Island.

"By comparing these accounts together, we may observe the variation does not alter very much hereabout; and although they differ about 7° of longitude in their reckonings from the Cape (which is not to be wondered at in so long a run, when sometimes they shall differ half as much on board the same ship), yet they agree as near as can be expected in their run from thence to Java Head; so that we may conclude that the difference of meridians between this island and Java Head be about 7°20'.

"That it does not lie about 3° or 4° at most, from the Coast of New Holland, appears from the following reasons. The ship Prince of Wales, in 1738, the evening before they made this coast, (in the latitude of Cloate's Island) observed the variation 5°55'N.westerly, being then at the largest computation about 38 leagues from the land; also the said ship made but 4½° meridian distance from thence to the west end of Cambava, lying according to these charts, much about 12° to the eastward of Java Head, ... there remains 7°½ westing to Java Head."

In 1782 the Hydrographic Office published a chart of Tryal Rocks (fig. 8), with the following note: "A True Draught of the Tryall Rocks in the latitude 19°30' South they were discovered in the year 1718 by a Dutch Ship and afterward by a sloop sent from Batavia they lie 80 leags. West from the Coast of New-Holland." The Hydrographer for the E.E.I.C., Dalrymple, in his Memoir of a Chart of the Indian Ocean published in 1787, tried to sort out the problem, (see fig. 9), "...the Danish Account places Tryal Rocks, viz, by a good good Meridien Observation when They bore W 2 or 3 miles, Lat. 20°40'S, M.23°45'E from St. Pauls; but by the run afterwards S ¼ W, 840' from Java Head.

"The Danish Account says, 'These Rocks lye NW and SE, and extend in length about 6 Dutch miles (24'), the centre of them appears very broad, and not higher out of the water than a small Vessels Hull: the Extremes are

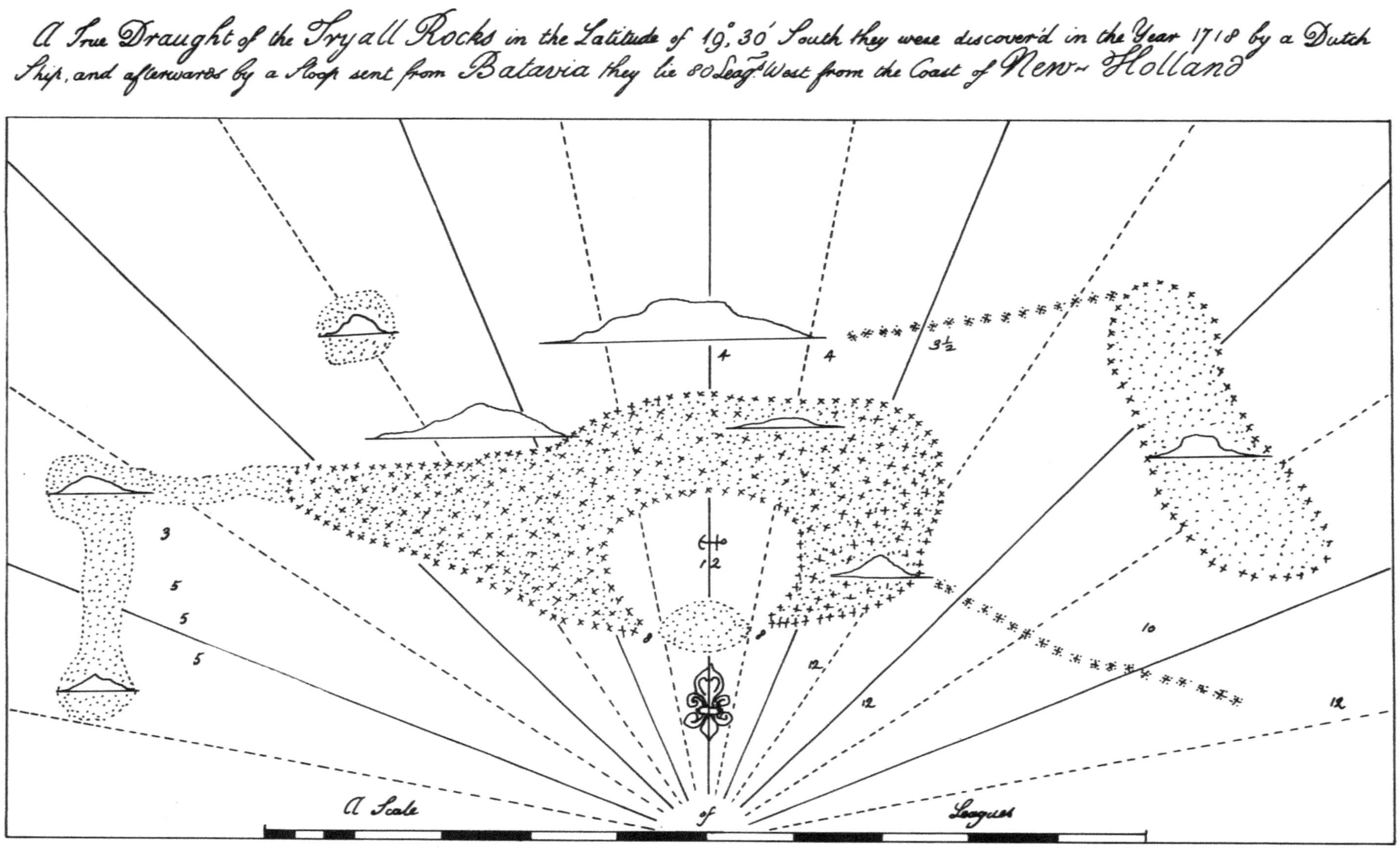
A True Draught of the Tryall Rocks in the Latitude of 19°, 30' South they were discover'd in the Year 1718 by a Dutch Ship, and afterwards by a Sloop sent from Batavia they lie 80 Leag.s West from the Coast of New~ Holland
4
4
3½
3
5
5
5
12
12
12
10
12
8
8
A Scale of Leagues

Fig. 8 Hydrographic Office Draught of Tryall Rocks after Dutch Plan of 1718.

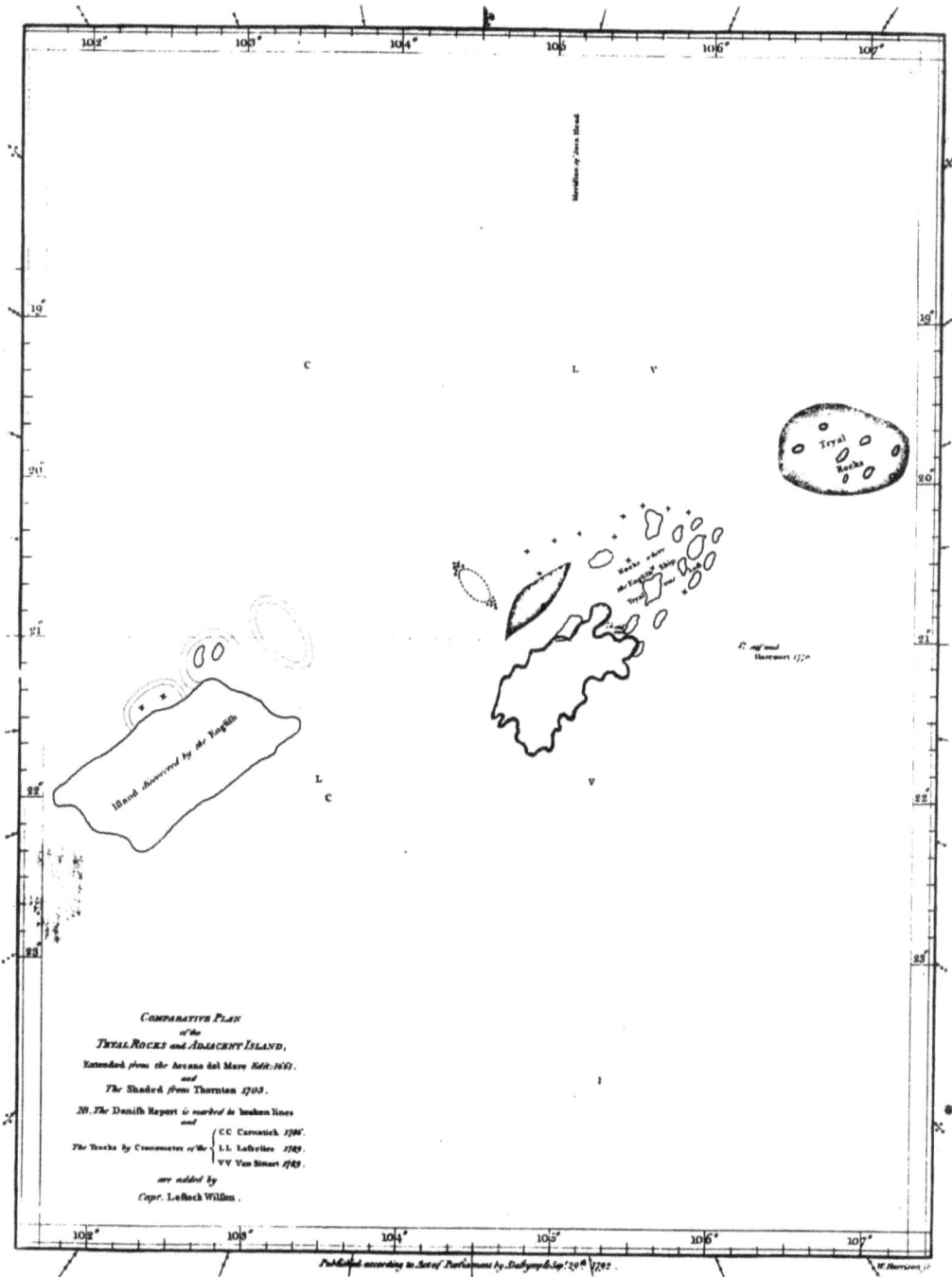

Fig. 9   Dalrymple's comparative Plan of Tryal Rocks.

clusters of small broken Rocks, now and then appearing, as the Sea retires, and are about 1 Dutch mile (4') from each extreme of the Main Rock, which is about 4 or 5 Dutch miles (16' or 20') in length.'

"I think there is reason to question, whether these be really the Tryal Rocks? for the Dutch Plan, made by a Sloop sent from Batavia, in consequence of a Dutch Ship having seen them in 1718, marks none of them, in particular, of nearly that extent; and describes the whole range lying E and W above 40 miles long in 19°30'S, 80 leagues from the Coast of New Holland (fig. 8). John Thornton, Edition 1703, in Lists of Latitudes, lays the Tryal Rocks in 19°45'S, and Seller in 1675 says, 'The dangerous Rocks called the Tryals, lye near upon the Latitude of 20°S (which Rocks take the name from one of our East India Ships that was lost thereupon, called the Tryal).' (note: this Event is said to have happened in 1622, but I can find no Traces of this Ship's Journal). His Chart of the World makes it in 130°E. from Teneriff, and about 20°E. from St. Pauls.

"Thornton, in his account of them, literally copies Seller but his Chart of the West Coast of New Holland, etc. he distinguishes the Tryal Rocks, which he places in Lat. from 19°30' to 20°5' S. (Mean Lat. 19°47'S.), and from 1°20' to 2°12'E. of Java Head. But beside them he lays down a large Island, 30 leagues distant from them to the SW½S; This Island extending nearly NE and SW 20 leagues: This he places from Latitude 20°48' to 21°30'S, and from 0°40' W to 0°30'E of Java Head: He also marks a Shoal, detached from the NW Coast about 5 leagues, from Lat. 20°30'S, and to 21°S, and from the Meridian of Java Head 0°30'W. (fig. 9).

"Not having the Journal of the Danish Ship Fredensberg Slott, Capt. Mathias Zosp, 1777, I cannot tell whether it was the NE part of this island in 21°S Lat. and the Shoal in 20°30'S, that they saw; but the extent of that, is about the length and direction which they describe the principal Rock to be; but what is meant by a Rock of 20' extent, I confess myself incompetant to say." Dalrymple, 1787.

At the start of the 19th century, we find a variety of islands appearing in the area off the N.W. Cape. The printed charts of Reinecke in 1801 and also Mortier Covens en Fils 1808 show Cloate's Island in about lat. 21°S., W. by S. of Trial Rocks which are shown in the meridian of the western point of Java. Another 'mystery' island is Bally Island S.S.E. of Trial Rocks in about lat. 22°S. On the chart by the geographer to the King, William Faden, published in 1817 and entitled, "A Chart of the India Ocean", Cloate's Island is shown S.W. of N.W. Cape and in longitude 8°E. of Java Head, with a note: "Discd. by Capt. Nash 1719 and observed by Capt. C. Christie of the Belvidere, 1796 but still doubted." Trial Rocks are shown in longitude of the W. point of Java, with a note: "Trial Rocks discovered by the Dutch 1718 (uncertain)."

In another chart by Lapie, published in 1812, Bally and Cloate's Islands are shown to the east of Trial Rocks, so that there seemed to be considerable doubt as to the position of all of these islands. In fact, by 1802, after Matthew Flinders had failed to find the rocks, the Admiralty Hydrographic Office declared that Trial Rocks did not exist.

In 1818, the brig <u>Greyhound</u> came upon a shoal in about lat. 20°S. This shoal was in fact the true Trial Rocks, but was not identified for at the time they were believed to be either non-existent or far to the west. James Horsburgh (1836), in his India Directory or Directions for sailing to and from the East Indies, China and Australia, described the Greyhound's Shoal as follows: "... discovered by the brig of that name bound from Calcutta to Batavia and Port Jackson, was seen 15th January 1818, at noon while observing; the breakers bearing from S.E.¾ E. by S.½S. distance 6 miles and extending about N.E. and S.W. an opening was observed in the middle of the shoal, no part of which appeared above the water, but the breakers were high. Our noon observations made the body of the shoal in lat. 19°58' S. long. 114°40½'E." The <u>Greyhound</u> arrived at Sydney on 14 April 1818 (Sydney Gazette: 18 April 1818), the master being listed as Captain Ritchie.

There is a series of curious letters in the newspapers in the following years which relate to Ritchie's Reef and are worth recording. In the Sydney Gazette, 18 March, 1820: "Captain Campbell, on his passage from China in the brig <u>Greyhound</u> discovered a reef extending E. and W. in Lat. 19°59'S. and Long. 103°30'E. which he supposes to be the Tryal Rocks, so long sought-after by different navigators." A week later the Gazette, published the following letter: "Sir, Observing in your last Gazette notice of a shoal discovered by the brig <u>Greyhound,</u> on her passage from China, I hand you an account of one discovered on a former voyage from Calcutta to this port. No doubt an insertion in your gazette will oblige. Yours Hatchway, Pipes and Co. (Extract from the brig <u>Greyhound's</u> Log Book). Course S.W.½W. wind N.W. at noon observed breakers bearing S.E.¾ E. to E. by S.½S. distance 7 or 8 miles, laying in a S.W. and N.E. direction. Lat. observations 20°15'S. long. per lunar observation 104°40' 18"E. The shoal appeared to extend about 5 miles in the above direction with rocks visible as the sea broke over them. The shoal appeared to have a clear opening in the centre, which might have been called two separate shoals. On seeing the shoals sounded 27 fathoms, sand, stone and broken shells; ship goin 3½ knots, 2 p.m. shoal visible from the mast head; sounded in 42 fathoms soft mud and clay, 6 p.m. sounded no ground in 62 fathoms, shoal not in sight; ship steering S.W."

A further letter to the Gazette published soon after this shows how easily Trial Rocks could be misplaced by about 560 n. miles (10°long.) due to a transcription error. Sydney Gazette, 1 April, 1820: "Sir, I beg leave to contradict the statement inserted by your last week's paper, enclosing a spurious extract from my log book, which only displays the ignorance and presumption of the writer; who under assumed names, has thought proper to contradict the truly respectable authority of so old a commander, and well-known and excellent a navigator as Captain W. Campbell. I myself enclose to you now, Sir, a true extract from my own log book; by which you will perceive that the shoal discovered by me lies close to the Coast of New Holland, the longitude of the ship at the time the bearings of the shoal were taken being 114°40'18" E. Lat. 20°15'S. I now leave it to Messrs. Hatchway, Pipes and Co. to ascertain the position of the Shoal, which I take it will find them sufficient employment for the next twelve months, when I request the pleasure of being favoured with a result of their calculations. I am Sir, Your obedient Servant, Thomas Ritchie.

Fig. 10   Lort Stoke's Plan of Tryal Rocks, Ritchie's Reef and Monte Bello
Islands.

'Moderate breeze and clear weather. At noon breakers bearing S.E. ' E. to E. by S.$\frac{1}{2}$S. and lying on a S.W. to N.E. direction: distance 6 miles, Lat. observed 20°15'S, - Long. from the mean of two sets of lunars 114°40'18"E.'" No doubt Hatchway, Pipes and Co. were somewhat put out by this letter, and their mistake of the longitude (104°40'18"E.); and nothing further was heard of the matter. The position of the centre of Ritchies' Reef is, therefore, lat. 20°18'S. Long. 114°45'52"E.

On 30 October 1820, Lt. Phillip Parker King in the brig Bathurst again passed through the area and observed: "... at 10 O'Clock we were in the latitude assigned to the Tryal Rocks by the brig Greyhound." After examining previous writings, they identified Bedout Island as that sighted by the Dutch sloop in 1718, and those sighted in July 1777 by the Danish Captain Matthias Foss in the Fredensberg Slot, in lat. 20°14'S. (lying N.W. and S.E. 24 miles) as the Monte Bello Islands. King concludes: "There can be no doubt that Barrow Island and Trimouille (which the French called the Monte Bello Islands) are the long-lost Trials." (Conrad 1969).

Finally Lt. Lort Stokes in H.M.S. Beagle charted Trial Rocks between the Monte Bello Islands and Barrow Island during his survey of the area between 31 August and 10 September, 1840, (fig. 10). Trial Rocks remained in this position and Ritchie's Reef remained off the N.W. of the Monte Bello Islands, until the publication of Ms. Ida Lee's article (1934): "The First Sighting of Australia by the English". Although it mentions Brookes' and Bright's letters, it says in the conclusion: "Since King's day naval surveyors have found their exact position. Admiralty Sailing Directions (1917) states: 'Tryal Rocks awash at high water are near the outer edge of the S.W. part of Monte Bello Islands reef and 5 miles N. of the North extreme of Barrow Island.' "

The modern Australia Pilot (1972) states: "Tryal Rocks (20°16'S., 115° 23'E.) consists of two coral heads, the S. of which dries 2.7 m, situated about 9 miles N.W. of Monte Bello Islands; the surrounding reefs are steep-to and can be approached to within a distance of $\frac{1}{2}$ mile." Australia Pilot, (1972), Vol. 5: 140.

14. THE DISCOVERING OF THE WRECKSITE

In 1969, a group of Perth skindivers, under the leadership of Mr. E. Christiansen and including Dr. N. Haimson and Messrs. E. R. Robinson and D. Nelly, visited the Trial Rocks to try and locate the wrecksite of the Trial. Within a few hours of starting the underwater search, a wrecksite was located on the western side of the south-western group of rocks. The wrecksite consisted of a number of iron cannon and anchors, and various small artifacts including a bronze pulley wheel (fig. 11), two pieces of lead (fig. 12) and an iron object. The circumstantial evidence seemed to indicate that the wrecksite was that of the Trial, a view not without its dissentients. The Western Australian Museum, under the terms of the Museum Act (Maritime Archaeology), paid an ex-gratia payment of Aust$2000 to the group for their work.

There followed in June and October of that year, two brief expeditions to

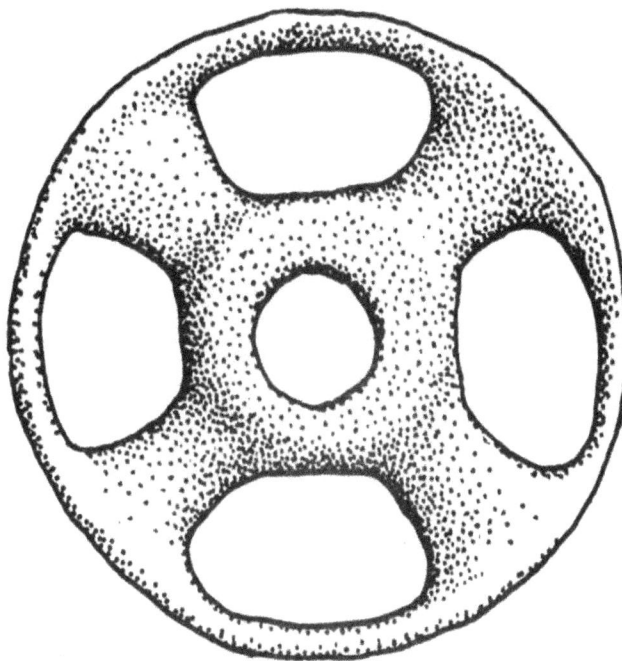

T968

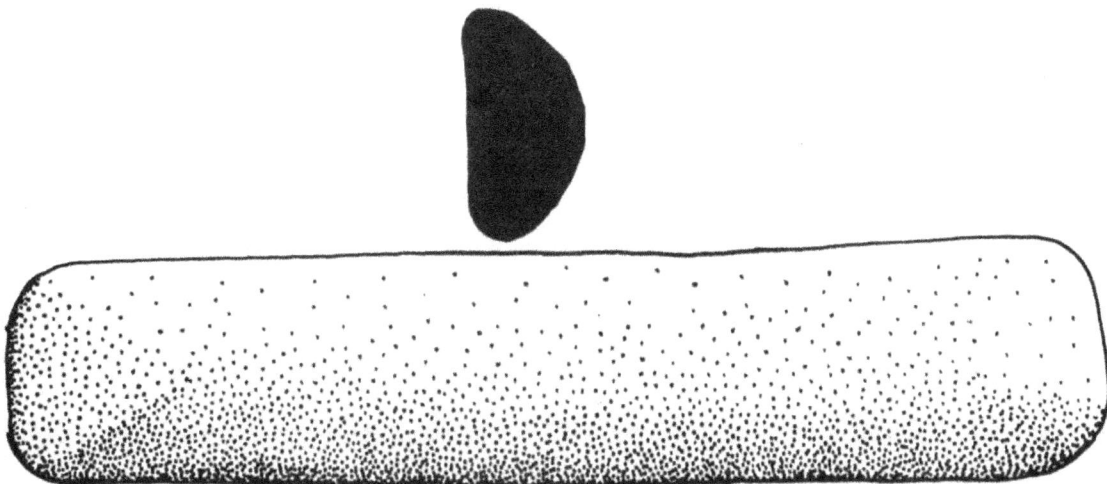

T339

Fig. 11   Bronze Pulley wheel.

Fig. 12   Lead ingot.

the site to recover material to help in identification of the site. Due to bad weather conditions (of a total 27 days only 5 hours diving on the site was possible), all that was recovered were ballast stones and an anchor fluke.

In June 1971, an expedition was mounted by the Museum sponsored by Mr. M. G. Kailis, managing director of Gulf Fisheries, together with members of the original discovery team. The objectives were to survey the site and to carry out a feasibility study for future excavation.

The wrecksite comprised two areas: the main section, on the western side of a large sand gully (fig. 13); and a smaller site near the rocks and on the eastern side of the sand gully. Heavy swell conditions prevented inspection of the latter site. The main part, an area 30 m long by 10 m wide, contained cannon and anchors. There were few small artefacts other than lead shot and scraps of lead sheet. The material all lies on rock and there appeared to be little concretion or buried matter. A photomosaic was made to show the general layout of the site and the distribution of cannon and anchors. Because of a heavy surge underwater, photographic conditions were not ideal. Systematic runs of overlapping vertical photographs were difficult to take, since the surge carried the photographer backwards and forwards for distances of up to 25 m. The mosaic only covers a part of the main site and some of the cannon could not be covered due to their exposed situation. However, an accurate plan of each cannon and anchor ($\pm$ 5%) was made from the mosaic (figs. 14 & 15) and it is estimated that the overall accuracy for the site plan is $\pm$ 10% approximately. For details of this recording technique see Green et al. (1971) and Baker and Green (1976).

15. THE IDENTIFICATION OF THE WRECKSITE

The documentary evidence indicates that present day Trial Rocks, is the site where the Trial was lost. However, it is difficult to ascertain if the wrecksite is that of the Trial. Identification of a wrecksite is always difficult, particularly where there is no local written tradition. It is easy, for example, to identify the wrecksite of the V.O.C. ship Amsterdam, lost within sight of Hastings in 1748. The wreck was well documented by contemporary observers (see Marsden 1974) and the site of the wreck is remembered through oral tradition today. Similarly, with the Armada ship Santa Maria de la Rosa, (Martin 1975), lost in Blasket Sound, Eira, in 1588, there was documentary evidence to indicate the wrecksite. After a long search a wrecksite was located; a pewter plate engraved with the name of a man known to have been on board, finally produced conclusive evidence for identification.

However, wrecks on the Western Australian coastline, lacking substantiation by any locally recorded documentary evidence before settlement (1829), have been identified from the records of survivors (where they existed), and from dateable artefacts found on the wreck. The V.O.C. ship Batavia (Drake-Brockman and Drok 1963, and Green 1975) was originally thought to have been lost in the Southern Group of the Houtman Abrolhos. Captain Lort Stokes, commander of H.M.S. Beagle, surveyed much of the coast of Western Australia in 1840, and identified correctly the Zeewijk site and incorrectly the Batavia and Trial sites. Finding wreckage on the southern island of the

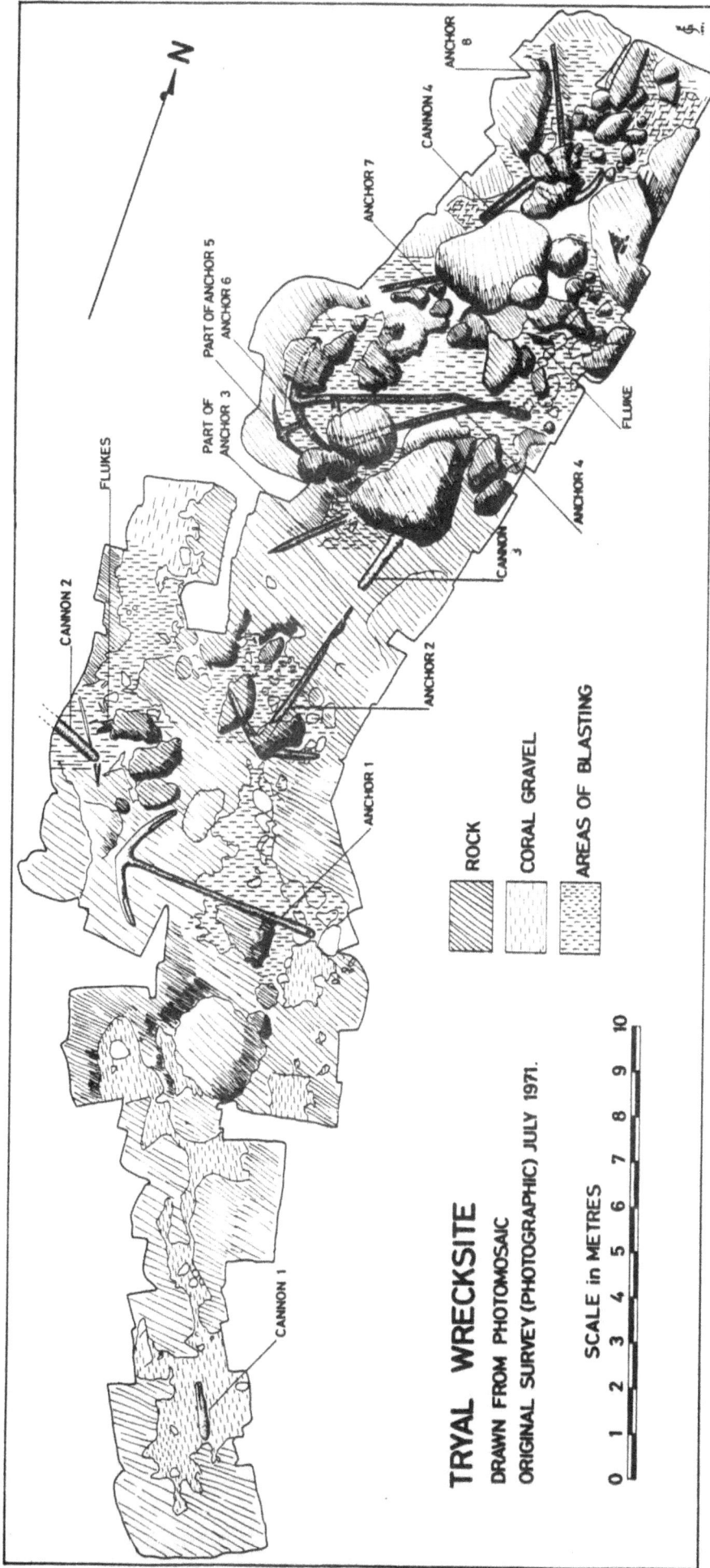

Fig. 13   Photomosaic of wrecksite, taken from original photographic survey, July 1971; scale in metres.

CANNON 2

CANNON 1

CANNON 3

CANNON 4

CANNON 5

0   METRE   1

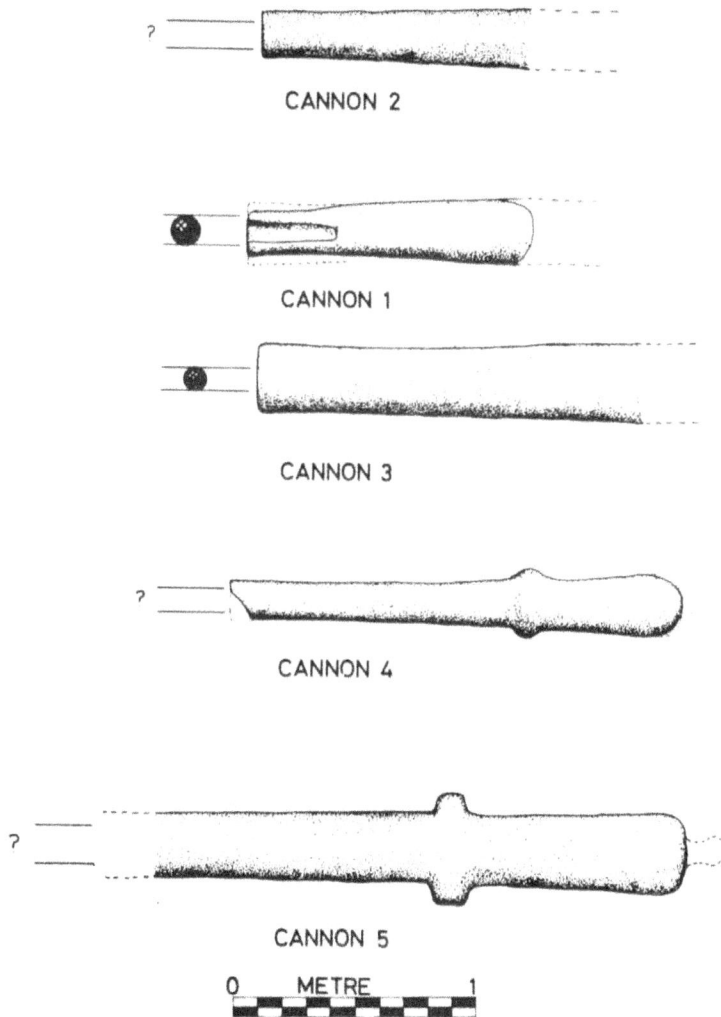

Fig. 14   Iron cannon from the wrecksite, showing their size and shape, from
photogrammetric survey, July 1971; scale 1 metre.

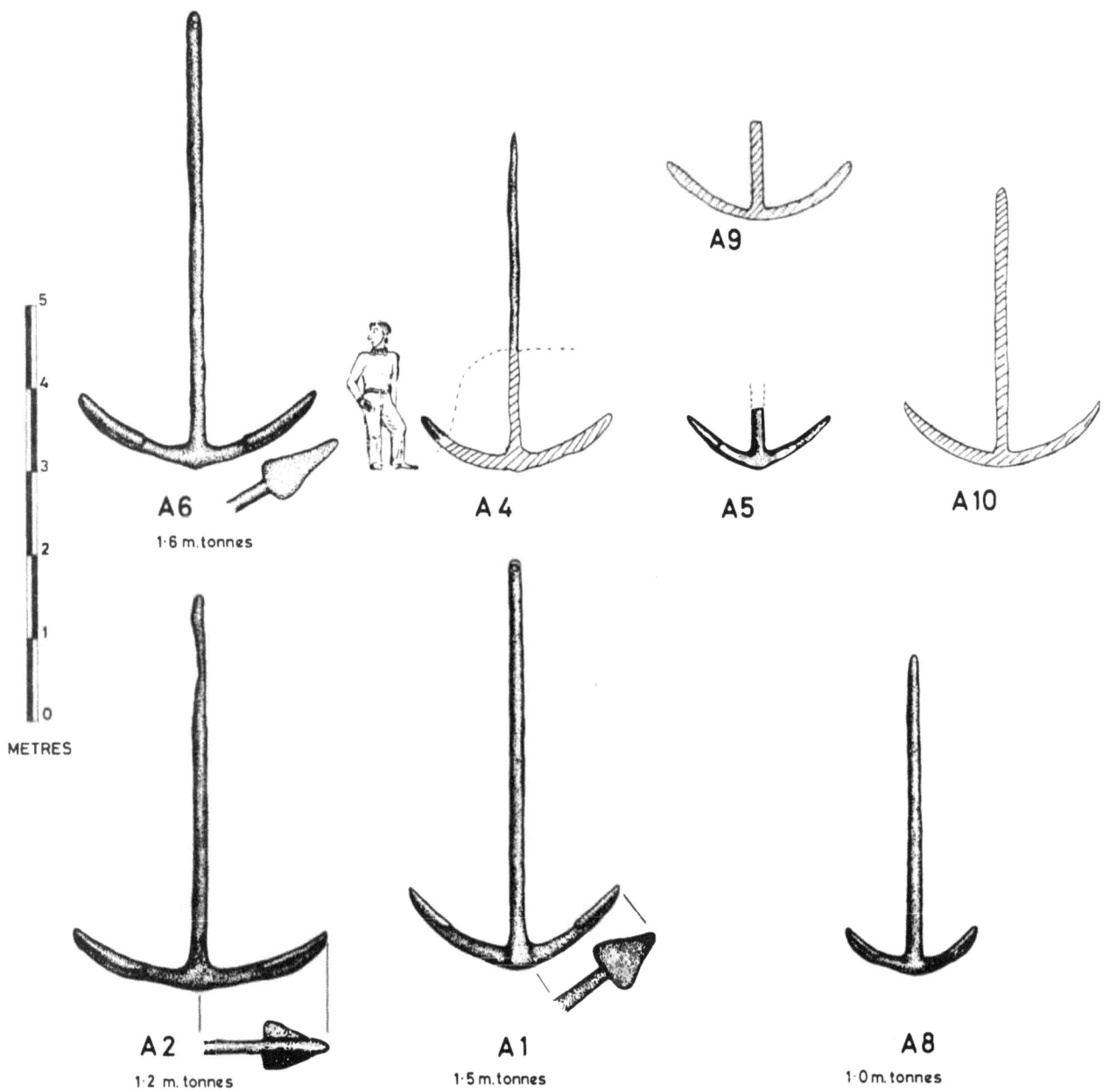

A9

A6
1·6 m. tonnes

A4

A5

A10

METRES

A2
1·2 m. tonnes

A1
1·5 m. tonnes

A8
1·0 m. tonnes

Fig. 15   Anchors from wrecksite, showing size and approximate weight,
hatched areas uncertain, A9 and A10 measured but not photographed,
scale 5 metres.

Southern Group of the Houtman Abrolhos, Stokes concluded that the Batavia was wrecked on the southern end of Half Moon Reef. He named various features there after the Batavia incident. In 1959, Miss Henrietta Drake-Brockman published extracts of Commandeur Francisco Pelsaert's journal of the loss of the Batavia and correctly concluded that the ship was lost on the Wallabi Group (Drake-Brockman and Drok 1963). In 1963, a wrecksite was located in that group on Morning Reef, and this was identified as being a V.O.C. ship (from the AVOC markings on the cannon), dated pre-1629 (from the coinage and dates on the cannon), and thus almost certainly that of the Batavia.

The V.O.C. jacht Vergulde Draeck was lost in 1656 on this coast around latitude 31⁰ 16'S. Seven survivors reached Batavia in the ship's boat, but the others who had reached the shore were never seen again. In 1963, a wreck was located in latitude 31⁰13'S and again from the AVOC marking and the dates on coins (found no later than 1655), it was concluded that this was the wrecksite of the Vergulde Draeck, (Green 1973).

The Zuytdorp was wrecked on Endrachtsland in 1712 with no survivors, thus the V.O.C. had no idea where the vessel was lost. In 1927 a stockman, Mr. Pepper discovered wreckage at the foot of the cliffs, north of the mouth of the Murchison River. The wrecksite material found on the cliffs was identified by Dr. P. E. Playford in 1960 as more than likely coming from the wreck of the Zuytdorp, a ship of the Zeeland chamber of the V.O.C. The coins were dated 1711 and the schellingen and dubbele stuivers were marked Zeeland with the Middelberg Mint mark. It was known that the entire minting of these coins from the Middelberg mint for that year were sent to the Indies in the Zuytdorp. Thus it was proven from the artefacts alone that the wreck was that of the Zuytdorp, (Playford 1959).

The Zeewijk was lost on Half Moon Reef in the Southern Abrolhos in 1727. The survivors spent about 8 months on the islands building another ship to take them to Batavia. Two of their charts of the area still survive, and there are contemporary descriptions of the loss. When Captain Stokes visited the islands he found a small swivel gun on one which he named Gun Island. He correctly concluded that the near-by Half Moon Reef was the site of the Zeewijk, lost in 1727 (Edwards 1970).

Henderson deals with the problem of the identification of the Cottesloe wreck near Perth. On examination of the artefacts associated with the wrecksite, and the historical evidence, Henderson provides convincing evidence that the site was not a 17th or 18th century vessel as was thought at first, but the wreck of a post-settlement vessel, the Elizabeth, lost in 1839 (Henderson 1973).

In the case of the Trial, the contemporary account of the loss (as has been shown) clearly indicates Trial Rocks as the area where the Trial was lost. However, the expedition that initially located the wrecksite searched only a very small part of the extensive reefs and no dated or easily dateable artefacts have been found on the wrecksite. Thus some consideration must be given to the evidence for the wrecksite being that of the Trial.

Firstly, the position of the wrecksite, on the S.W. corner of the S.W. group of rocks is consistent with the Trial's course (see discussion above). The ship was on a N.E. course (Brookes) and N.E. by E. (Bright) from a position N.W. of N.W. Cape, when she struck, and this would have put the Trial in the vicinity of the present day wrecksite.

The wrecksite examined and recorded during the 1971 expedition, includes five iron cannon and eight anchors, together with some scraps of lead sheeting, and a few small lead shot. Earlier expeditions recorded possibly two more cannons and two more anchors in areas that could not be reached during the 1971 expedition because of the sea conditions. Further artefacts recovered include a small lead ingot and a brass-bronze pulley wheel.

The cannons (fig. 14) are extremely eroded and difficult to identify in size or type. The number of cannons, at least seven (perhaps one or two more), is of interest, because it tends to indicate a small ship, or at least a lightly armed one. Since there is no record of E.E.I.C. gun establishments for the period, nor is there any indication of the size of the Trial or the number of guns she carried, it is difficult to draw any conclusions. However, the V.O.C. had clearly defined gun ratings for various ship sizes. Van Dam (1701) states that a small jagt in 1632 of 100 Amst. voet carried 8 iron guns firing 3 to 4 Amst. lb. shot. In this period 100 Amst. voet vessel was about 100 tons displacement. This tends to indicate that the ship was small, compared with the E.E.I.C. ship Moone (see above) which had 59 guns.

Nonetheless, the number and size of anchors on the wrecksite tend to indicate a much larger vessel, although it is possible that the Trial was carrying anchors for the E.E.I.C. ships in the Indies. However, there is no documentary evidence for this. The largest anchor A6 is 5.5 metres long (fig. 15), and is presumably the sheet anchor; anchors A1 and A2 are both about 5 m long and are probably bower anchors. The anchors appear to be slim for their size but very large. An approximate estimate of their weight (for they are badly eroded), gives A6 = 1.6 tonnes, A1 = 1.5 tonnes, A2 = 1.2 tonnes and A8 = 1 tonne.

Examining four different 17th century sources for the proportions of an anchor, together with size and number in relation to the size of the vessel, we may draw some conclusions as to the possible size of the vessel.

Manwayring (1644) states in his Seaman's Dictionary: "Anchor: .... The proportion which it holds in it selfe is, The shanke is thrice as long as one of the flookes, and half the beam. The proportion in respect of shipping is, to a Ship of 500 tun, we allow 2000 weight for a sheate Anchor, The biggest Ship in Englands anchor is but 3500 ...." It may be seen that the anchors on this wrecksite would tend to indicate a ship of at least 500 tun according to Manwayring, but the proportions do not agree, the shank being longer than 3 times the flukes and half the beam.

Witsen (1690) reckons in his Architectura Navalis et Regimen Nauticum that twice the thickness of schacht (shank) of an anchor in Amsterdam duimen expressed in Amsterdam voeten plus the product in duimen gives the length. Thus for a thickness of 6A.duim; 2 x 6 = 12 voet + 12 duim = 13 voet 1 duim (11A.duim = 1A.voet) (below 500 pondt weight of anchor, three times thickness gives length). Furthermore three times the thickness of the schacht in duimen plus two noughts gives its weight in Amsterdam pondt. Thus a thickness of 6 duimen gives: 6 x 3 = 18 + 00 = 1800 A. lb. Witsen gives a table (table 1) which tabulates length of schacht against thickness and weight, that does not exactly agree in some instances with the proportions given in the text. The Amsterdam pondt = 0.4948 kg thus roughly by proportion,anchor A6 would weigh about 1106 kg. Witsen also writes that for a ship 100 A.voet in length 1000 A.lb anchor is usual, and for every additional 10A.voet of the ship's length, 100A.lb. weight is added, thus implying the Trial would be 254 A.voet long. However, there were variations, since he later quotes an Oost-Indisch Schip 170 A.voet long with an anchor of 3300 A.lbs.

Van IJk (1697) has a different formula in De Nederlandsche Scheeps-Bouw-Konst. He says that the weight of an anchor is the cube of the schagt (shank) in A.voet, but notes that sometimes anchors with the same length of schagt could vary between 3000 and 5000 A.lb. Van IJk also gives a table (table 2) of the relationship between the width of a ship, and the length and weight of corresponding anchors, (added to the table is the corresponding length of a ship, from elsewhere in van IJk). Thus van IJk would seem to indicate that from the size of its anchors, the wreck was of one of the largest class of ships.

Van Dam (1701) in his Beschrijvinge van der Oostindische Compagnie, gives the specification for anchors given by the Heren XVII for three types of V.O.C. ship for the year 1697 (table 3). It may be seen here that the V.O.C. ships, certainly in the late 17th century, according to the Resolutions of the Heren XVII, had heavier anchors than Witsen states. Notwithstanding, the available documentary information for the 17th century implies from the anchors on the wrecksite that the ship was of a very large class.

The main wrecksite has ten anchors and five cannon. These were surveyed during the 1971 expedition, however, the original finders reported in 1969, that this site had ten anchors and eleven cannon. Unfortunately, the finders made no plans of the wrecksite at the time and the two subsequent survey expeditions did not produce any plans or survey details. The other concentration of material to the east of the main site was said to have five cannon and five anchors. Thus according to the finders the wrecksite has fifteen anchors and sixteen cannon, but this should be treated with some caution.

The main site with ten anchors, five cannon and a considerable quantity of granite ballast appears to represent the main part of the ship. The granite ballast indicates that the vessel was not a 17th century V.O.C. ship, which usually carried brick ballast (Batavia, Drake-Brockman and Drok 1963, Green 1975; Vergulde Draeck, Green 1973; Lastdrager, Sténuit 1974; Kennermerlandt, Aston Univ. S.A.C. 1974, Price and Muckelroy 1974; etc.).

The group of three anchors approximately in the centre of the wrecksite is typical of several wrecks of East Indiamen. The Batavia 1629 (Green 1975) has a similar group of 4 anchors in the centre of the wrecksite. From the way the Batavia appears to have fallen over on her starboard side, it may be concluded that the anchors were stored upright in the hold, unstocked with their crown down. Boudriot (1973) Planche 21, shows in the longitudinal section of the Vaisseau de 74 Cannons, one replacement anchor stored unstocked in the hold, crown up. The Hollandia, 1743 (Cowan, Cowan & Marsden 1975), has a cluster of three anchors like that of the Batavia in which

TABLE 1

WITSEN

Eeen korte afdeelinge van Ankers lengte, dikte, en zwaarte

$13\frac{1}{2}$ voet l.	$6\frac{1}{3}$ ($\frac{3}{4}$?) duim dik	2000 pont zw.
$13\frac{1}{4}$	$6\frac{1}{2}$	1900
13	6	1800
$12\frac{3}{4}$	$5\frac{3}{4}$	1700
$12\frac{1}{2}$	$5\frac{1}{2}$	1600
12	5	1500
$11\frac{3}{4}$	$4\frac{3}{4}$	1400
$11\frac{1}{2}$	$4\frac{1}{2}$	1300
$11\frac{1}{4}$	$4\frac{1}{4}$	1200
11	4	1100
$10\frac{3}{4}$	$3\frac{3}{4}$	1000
$10\frac{1}{2}$	$3\frac{1}{2}$	900
$10\frac{1}{4}$	$3\frac{1}{4}$	800
10	$3\frac{1}{6}$	700
$9\frac{3}{4}$	3	600
9	$2\frac{3}{4}$	500
8	$2\frac{1}{2}$	400
7	$2\frac{1}{4}$	300
6	2	200
5	$1\frac{3}{4}$	100

TABLE 3

Van Dam

't Gewigte en't getal der anckers

Met een schip van 160 voet werden medegeven 9 anckers, wegen als volgt	Met een schip van 140 voet werden medegeven 8 anckers, wegen als volgt	Met een schip van 130 voet werden medegeven 7 anckers, wegen als volgt
3600 pont	3000 pont	2200 pont
3500	2900	2100
3400	2800	2050
3300	2700	2000
3200	2600	650
3100	750	600
900	700	130
850	160	
180		

TABLE 2

Van IJk

(Length of ship)	Een schip wijd	't Anker lang	't Anker
	8 voeten	$3\frac{1}{5}$ voeten	33 ponden zwaar
	9	$3\frac{3}{5}$	47
	10	4	64
	11	$4\frac{2}{5}$	84
	12	$4\frac{4}{5}$	110
	13	$5\frac{1}{2}$	140
	14	$5\frac{3}{5}$	175
60 voeten	15	6	216
64	16	$6\frac{2}{5}$	262
68	17	$6\frac{4}{5}$	314
72	18	$7\frac{2}{5}$	373
76	19	$7\frac{3}{5}$	439
80	20	8	512
84	21	$8\frac{2}{5}$	592
88	22	$8\frac{4}{5}$	681
92	23	$9\frac{1}{5}$	778
96	24	$9\frac{3}{5}$	884
100	25	10	1000
104	26	$10\frac{2}{5}$	1124
108	27	$10\frac{4}{5}$	1259
112	28	$11\frac{1}{5}$	1405
116	29	$11\frac{3}{5}$	1562
120	30	12	1728

Table 2 (continued)

(Length of ship)	Een schip wijd	't Anker lang	't Anker
124	31	$12\frac{2}{5}$	1906
128	32	$12\frac{4}{5}$	2097
132	33	$13\frac{1}{5}$	2300
136	34	$13\frac{3}{5}$	2515
140	35	14	2742
144	36	$14\frac{2}{5}$	2986
148	37	$14\frac{4}{5}$	3242
152	38	$15\frac{1}{5}$	3512
156	39	$15\frac{3}{5}$	3796
160	40	16	4096
164	41	$16\frac{2}{5}$	4426
168	42	$16\frac{4}{5}$	4742
172	43	$17\frac{1}{5}$	5088
176	44	$17\frac{3}{5}$	4551
180	45	18	5832

the crowns are all facing the same direction and located roughly in the centre of the site. The number of anchors on the Hollandia site is interesting because there was no contemporary salvage work carried out although she may have lost some anchors before she sank. As far as we know from Pelsaert's journal, no anchors were recovered in salvage work carried out on the Batavia at the time the loss. Thus the number and distribution of the anchors on the Batavia represent the original number carried and their approximate position. (Table 4 gives the number and size of anchors on the wrecksites of the Hollandia, Trial and Batavia for comparative purposes.)

It is interesting to note that the Association which was lost in 1707, carried anchors with 5.59 m-long shanks, 250 mm thick, which correspond quite closely in shape with the Trial anchors. The Association was 50 m long and had 1483 tonne displacement (Morris 1969).

The small bronze pulley sheaf is inconclusive for dating purposes. Manwayring (1644): "Sheevers. There are two sorts of Sheevers used, either of brasse or wood; the brasse sheevers are now little used but in the heeles of the top-masts: the wooden sheevers are either one whole peece; and these they use for all small pullies, and small blocks; but in the knights and winding-tackles-blocks, they use sheevers which are made of quarters of wood let into each other; for these will hold when the whole Sheevers will split, and are called quarter-sheevers." Röding (1796) also mentions bronze pulley sheeves.

Large bronze sheaves were found on the wreck of Association, lost in the Scilly Isles in 1707. These had five square spokes (Morris 1969), and appear to be 3 or 4 times the size of the Trial sheaves.

A number of fine grey granite blocks were noted on the wrecksite, ranging in size up to 0.3 m square. Since granite is not a local rock, these blocks are thought to be ballast. The presence of this type of ballast and the lack of bricks indicates that the vessel was not a V.O.C. ship outward bound to the Indies, which typically carried bricks as a paying ballast. Bricks have been found on the wrecks of the V.O.C. ships Batavia (9000 bricks), Vergulde Draeck (8000 bricks) and Zeewijk (a few), that were lost on the coast of

TABLE 4

Anchors on Wrecksites of Hollandia, Batavia and Trial

Hollandia	Trial	Batavia
4.7 m sheet	5.5	4.5 sheet
3.7 m bower	5.0	4.25 bower
3.3 m bower	5.0	3.5 bower
3.3 m bower	4.0	3.5 bower
2.0 m stream	3.8	3.25 stream
2.3 m kedge	3.5	4.25 hold
?	?	4.25 hold
?	?	4.25 hold
		4.25 hold

Western Australia and on other wrecks of outward bound V.O.C. ships. Requisitions of the Gouverneur Generaal of the V.O.C. in the Indies to the company at home, indicate that in the mid-17th century large numbers of bricks were requested for building purposes in the Indies, (Koloniaal Archief 10072). For example, in the year 1654, 100000 Vries Clijnkert (Friesland Bricks), 100000 grauwe leijts moppen (grey Leiden bricks), 50000 leijts cleijne grauwe clijnkert (small grey Leiden bricks) and 50000 Goutse Clijnkert (gouda bricks) were requested. The Vergulde Draeck which arrived at Batavia in 1654 on her first voyage carried 26000 vries Clijnkert. It should be noted that these are the small yellow bricks, referred to by some authors (Forster and Higgs 1973) as Overijsselsde Steen, although in fact either IJsel steen, Goudse steen or Fries steen.

On final analysis, the evidence from the wrecksite does tend to be equivocal. Whereas nothing conclusively indicates that the wrecksite is not the Trial, the anchors tend to suggest a larger vessel than one would expect if this were the case; the ballast, that she was not V.O.C.; and the cannon, that she was a small ship.

Should another wrecksite with cannon and anchors be found on Trial Rocks, one would have to seriously reconsider the question of the wrecksite being that of the Trial. Until some dated or dateable artefact is discovered on the wrecksite, the identification is only tentative that the wrecksite is that of the Trial.

ACKNOWLEDGEMENTS

The author wishes to express his appreciation to the staff of the Department of Maritime Archaeology of the Western Australian Museum who participated in the 1971 expedition, together with Lt. Commander D. Lambert and P.O. T. Minchen of the Royal Australian Navy, Dr. J. Williams, Dr. N. Haimson and Mr. E. Christiensen. Thanks are due to the sponsor of the expedition Mr. M. Kailis, and to the Western Australian Petroleum Company who provided logistic support.

I would like to thank the numerous people who have helped with the preparation of this manuscript, particularly Susan Hogan and Patricia Brown. The author gratefully acknowledges the assistance of the Western Australian Museum and the Australian Research Grant Council.

REFERENCES

Aston University Sub-Aqua Club, (1974). The wreck of the Kennemerland. University of Aston, Birmingham.

Australia Pilot, (1972). North, north-west, and west coasts of Australia from the west entrance of Endeavour Strait to Cape Leeuwin. Vol. 5, 6th Edit., N.P. 17. Hydrographer of the Navy.

Baker, P.E. and Green, J. N., (1976). Recording Techniques used During the Excavation of the Batavia. Int. J. Naut. Arch., 5.2:143-158.

Blaeu, W. J., (1612). The Light of Navigation. Amsterdam.

Bontekoe, W. Y., (1646). Journal ofte Gedenck waerdighe beschrijvinghe vande Oost-Indische Reyse van Willem Ysbrantsz Bontekoe van Hoorn Begrijpende veel wonderlijcke en ghevaerlijcke saecken hem der in wedorvaren. Begonnenden 18 December 1618 en vol-eijnt den 16 November 1625. Hoorn 1646.

Boudriot, J., (1973). Le Vaisseau de 74 Cannons; Traité pratique d'art naval. Collections Archéologie Navale Francaise, Éditions des Quatre Seigneurs, Genoble.

Bourne, W., (1580). A Regiment for the Sea, Conteining very Necessary Matters, for all sorts of Sea-men and Travailers, as Masters of ships, pilots, mariners and merchauntes, newly corrected and ammended by the Author. London.

Colenbrander, H. T., (1923). Jan Peitersz Coen, Bescheiden omtrent zijn Bedrijf in Indië. den Haag, 1923.

Conrad, M., (1969). West Australia's "disappearing" rocks. The Countryman, 19 June, 1969.

Cowan, R., Cowan, Z. and Marsden, P. (1975). The Dutch East Indiaman Hollandia wrecked on the Isles of Scilly in 1743. Int. J. Naut. Arch., 4-2: 267-300.

van Dale, (1970). van Dale Groot Woordenboeck der Nederlandse Taal. Martinus Nijhoff, 's-Gravenhage.

Dalrymple, A., (1787). Memoir of a Chart of the Indian Ocean. London.

van Dam, P., (1701). Beschrijvinge van de Oostindische Compagnie. Ed. F. W. Stapel; Pieter van Dam's Beschrijvinge van der Oostindische Compagnie. Rijks Geschiedkundige Publicatiën. Martinus Nijhoff, 's-Gravenhage.

Drake-Brockman, H. and Drok, E.D., (1963). Voyage to Disaster, the Life of Francisco Pelsaert. Angus and Robertson, Sydney.

Dudley, R., (1661). Dell Arcano del Mare. Florence.

Dunn, S., (1780). A new Directory for the East Indies. London.

Edwards, H., (1970). Wreck on Half Moon Reef. Robert Hale, Sydney.

Forster, W. A. and Higgs, K. B., (1973). The Kennemerland, 1971, An interim report. Int. J. Naut. Arch. 2-2: 291-300.

Green, J. N., (1973). The wreck of the Dutch East Indiaman Vergulde Draeck, 1656. Int. J. Naut. Arch., 2-2: 267-289.

Green, J. N., (1975). The V.O.C. ship Batavia wrecked in 1629 on the Houtman Abrolhos, Western Australia. Int. J. Naut. Arch., 4-1: 43-64.

Green, J. N., Baker, P. E., Richards, B. and Squire, D. M., (1971). Simple Underwater Photogrammetric Techniques. Archaeometry, 13-2: 221-232.

Gunter, E., (1623). The description and use of the Sector, the crosse-staffe and other instruments. For such as are studious of mathematical practise. London.

Halls, C., (1964). Two plates: Being an account of the Dirk Hartog and Vlamingh Plates, their loss and subsequent recovery. Westerly, March 1964: 33-40.

Heeres, J. E., (1899). The Part Bourne by the Dutch in the Discovery of Australia, 1606-1765. Luzac, Amsterdam.

Henderson, G., (1973). The wreck of the Elizabeth. Studies in Historical Archaeology No. 1. Sydney.

Hewson, J. B., (1963). A History of the Practice of Navigation. Brown and Ferguson, Glasgow.

Horsburgh, J., (1836). India directory or directions for sailing to and from the East Indies, China and Australia (4th ed.) Allen, London.

van IJk, C., (1697). De Nederlandsche Scheeps bouw-konst. Amsterdam.

Irving, I. (ed.), (1936). Bligh and the Bounty. London.

Lee, Marriot, I., (1934). The first sighting of Australia by the English. Roy. Aust. Hist. Soc. J. and Proc., 20-5: 273-280.

Manwayring, H., (1644). The Sea-mans Dictionary or, an Exposition and demonstration of all the Parts and Things belonging to a Shippe. London.

Marsden, P., (1974). The wreck of the Amsterdam. Hutchinson, London.

Martin, C. J. M., (1972). The Adelaar: a Dutch East Indiaman wrecked on Barra, 1728. Underwater Association Scottish Symposium Report: 51-54.

Martin, C. J. M., (1975). Full Fathom Five: Wrecks of the Spanish Armada. Chatto and Windus, London.

Morris, R., (1969). Island Treasure: the search for Sir Cloudesley Shovell's flagship Association. Hutchinson, London.

Mörzer Bruyns, W. F. J. and Schilder, G., (1974). Kaarten en Stuurmange-
    reedschappen. Spiegel Historiael, 9.9: 478-486.

Norwood, R., (1637). The Sea-mans Practice, Contayning a Fundamentall
    Problem in Navigation, Experimentally verified. London.

Onions, C. T. (ed.), (1968). The Shorter Oxford English Dictionary on
    Historical Principles (3rd ed.) Clarendon Press, Oxford.

Playford, P. E., (1959). The wreck of the Zuytdorp on the Western Australian
    Coast in 1712. J. and Proc. W.A. Hist. Soc., 5-5: 5-41.

Price, R. and Muckelroy, K., (1974). The second season of work on the
    Kennemerland site, 1973. An interim report. Int. J. Naut. Arch.,
    3.2: 257-268.

Purchas, S., (1625). Hakluyt Posthumous or Purchas his Pilgrimes.
    Hakluyt Society Publications, Extra series, London.

Quinn, D. B., (1971). The Voyage of Triall 1606-1607: An Abortive
    Virginia Venture. Am. Neptune, 31-2: 85-103.

Raven-Hart, R., (1967). Before van Riebeeck: callers at South Africa from
    1488 to 1652. C. Struik, Cape Town.

Röding, J. H., (1796). Allgemeines Wörterbuch der Marine. Hamburg.

Sainsbury, W. N., (1870). Callendar of State Papers, (Colonial). P.R.O.,
    London.

Schilder, G., (1976). Australia Unveiled: the share of the Dutch navigators
    in the discovery of Australia. Theatrvm Orbis Terrarvm, Amsterdam.

Stapel, F. W., (1937). De Oostindische Compagnie en Australië. Patria, 4.
    Vaderlandsche Cultuurgeschiedenis in monografieën, van Kampen,
    Amsterdam.

Sténuit, R., (1974). Early relics of the V.O.C. trade from Shetland. The
    wreck of the flute Lastdrager lost off Yell, 1653. Int. J. Naut. Arch.,
    3.2: 213-256.

Strachan, M. and Penrose, B., (1971). The East India Company Journals of
    Captain William Keeling and Master Thomas Bonner, 1615-1617.
    University of Minnesota Press, Minneapolis.

Sigmond, J. P. and Zuiderbaan, L. H., (1976). Nederlanders Ontdekken
    Australië: Scheepsarcheologische vondsten op het Zuidland. De Boer
    Maritiem, Bussum.

Smith, J., (1627). A Sea Grammar. London.

Snellius, W., (1617). Eratosthenes Batavvs. Colster.

Valentijn, F., (1726). Oud-en Nieuw Oost-Indiën, In descriptioneum Indiae
    Orientalis. Dordrecht.

Wagenaar, L. J., (1583). The Mariners Mirrour, London.

Waters, D. W., (1958). The Art of Navigation in England in Elizabethan and Early Stuart Times. Hollis and Carter, London.

Witsen, N., (1690). Architectura Navalis et Regimen Nauticum ofte Aaloude en Hedendaagsche Scheeps-bouw en Bestier. Amsterdam.

Wright, E., (1599). Certain Errors in Navigation, arising either of the ordinarie erroneous making or using of the Sea Chart, compass, cross staffe and tables of declination of the Sunne and fixed starres detected and corrected. London.

www.ingramcontent.com/pod-product-compliance
Lightning Source LLC
Chambersburg PA
CBHW051309270326

41929CB00029B/3471